ACADEMIC
AUTHORITY

ACADEMIC
AUTHORITY

THE PROFESSOR'S GUIDE
TO BECOMING A SOUGHT-AFTER
THOUGHT LEADER

GREGORY UNRUH

Copyrighted Material

Academic Authority: The Professor's Guide to Becoming a Sought-After Thought Leader

Copyright © 2025 by Global Leadership Academy Press.
All Rights Reserved.

No part of this publication may be reproduced, stored in a retrieval system or transmitted, in any form or by any means—electronic, mechanical, photocopying, recording, or otherwise—without prior written permission from the publisher, except for the inclusion of brief quotations in a review.

For information about this title or to order other books and/or electronic media, contact the publisher:

Global Leadership Academy Press
Washington, DC
globalleadershipacademy.com

ISBNs:
978-1-7354671-2-2 (softcover)
978-1-7354671-3-9 (eBook)

Printed in the United States of America

Cover and Interior design: 1106 Design

For those fellow professors who have the curiosity and desire to leave an impactful legacy beyond the ivory tower.

Table of Contents

INTRODUCTION: Bridging the Relevance Gap	ix
PART I: The Foundations of Authority	1
1. A Tree Hugger in the Halls of Capitalism	3
2. The Authority Motivations and Lifestyle	13
3. The Authority Mindset	27
4. Authority Development Trajectory	51
PART II: The Authority Framework	63
5. The Authority Map	65
6. Connecting with Communities and their Concerns	69
7. Engaging in Value-added Conversations	85
8. Crafting Solutions to Practitioner Problems	105
9. Communicating Your Solutions	127
PART III: Beyond Authority: Capturing Value	147
10. An Authority Enterprise Beyond the Ivory Tower	149
11. Capturing Your Share of Your Created Value	155
AFTERWORD: Authority in a Complex World	181
ABOUT THE AUTHOR	183

Introduction
Bridging the Relevance Gap

*"The scientist is not a person who gives the right answers;
he's one who asks the right questions."*
—Claude Lévi-Strauss

I've met many academics whose scholarship gives them valuable insights that could positively impact managerial practice, but their message fails to reach the people who need it most. This book intends to remedy that situation.

Academic Authority: The Professor's Guide to Becoming a Sought-After Thought Leader is for academics who want to apply their expertise to real-world problems by reaching the executives leading today's top companies. Doing so can be personally and professionally fulfilling, as well as lucrative. More important, sharing relevant scholarly insights makes a valuable contribution to the practice of management, helping managers achieve their goals and ensure that their organizations benefit the marketplace and society.

If you are an academic looking to impact practice, now is a remarkable time. The barriers that once kept you from getting your ideas and messages out have collapsed. No longer do editors, publishers, meeting planners, and the like stand as gatekeepers. The tools to speak directly to your audience are freely and readily available. What was once an obscure and mysterious world of guru professors is now within reach of us all.

I base the advice in this book on my own experience in developing a successful authority trajectory. Mine was an improbable journey, riddled with mistakes. The good news? You can learn from my blunders and leapfrog the potholes I encountered.

But this book is not my story alone. I ground it with interviews I have had with leading academic authorities. These standout scholar-celebrities—faculty from leading institutions like the Wharton School at the University of Pennsylvania, the Tuck School at Dartmouth, Sloan School at MIT, and the Marshall School at USC—graciously shared their time and knowledge with me, and I feel privileged to share what I learned from them with you.

This book also builds off work I have done to create a Digital Leadership course at my home institution—George Mason University in Fairfax, Virginia, the state's largest public university—that teaches college students how to leverage the techniques of online influencers to advance causes they care about. I developed the course by drawing on my case writing and field research of leading motivational speakers, trainers, and influencers—including Tony Robbins, Deepak Chopra, Werner Erhardt, and others—many of whom I had direct and extended access to. I've tried to distill more than two decades of learning into this book. You will read about successes—and plenty of mistakes—all in service of helping you achieve your goals.

Three Core Assertions

I build my case on a foundation of three assertions about practitioner-focused work.

The first is:

1. *Practitioners face incessant waves of novel problems.*

   Trendy managerial shorthand for the shifting and unpredictable nature of modern business is VUCA, as in "It's a VUCA world out there!" VUCA—Volatility, Uncertainty, Complexity, and Ambiguity. Like some of the best

Introduction

acronyms, the term originated in the military (they also gave us FUBAR and SNAFU; you can look them up). But today VUCA applies to any organization seeking to navigate constant change.

In the last years, waves of VUCA change have included:

~ **A global health crisis**—The COVID-19 pandemic created unprecedented uncertainty with the rapid spread of the virus SARS-CoV-2, shifting scientific understanding, and emergency public-health measures that impacted and, in many cases, entirely shut down businesses.

~ **Societal shifts**—In 2020, movements like Black Lives Matter and #MeToo have increased scrutiny of workplace practices and systemic inequities. Companies that ignore these movements face backlashes from consumers and employees, while those taking decisive action alienate traditional stakeholders, impacting their reputations. Less than five years later, we've seen a backlash against DEI programs and ESG.

~ **Environmental change**—Natural disasters, including climate-induced hurricanes, floods, and wildfires, are on the rise. Companies must make long-term commitments amid uncertainty about the extent and rate of global change.

~ **Technological transformations**—The rise of Artificial Intelligence, automation, and associated innovations is transforming industries, fostering both job losses and skilled-worker shortages while upending the competitive landscape across sectors.

~ **Cybersecurity**—The growing frequency and sophistication of cybersecurity threats, data breaches, ransomware attacks, and the like have multiplied complexity for executives, absorbing increasing amounts of managerial attention.

~ **Geopolitics**—The wars in Ukraine and Gaza, populist political movements like MAGA and the UK Brexit decision, along with other events create far-reaching implications for trade, finance, and political relations. Tensions among the United States, China, Russia, Israel, Iran, and other countries create uncertainty around global supply chains, trade, tariffs, and regulations.

These and other challenges foster ongoing complexity and uncertainty for managers, which leads to the second assertion:

2. *To confront these challenges, executives need actionable guidance now.*
While existing academic theory can provide solid guidance, much academic work is ill-suited to helping executives confront the latest emergent challenges. While the scientific process can *eventually* provide a response, accumulating sufficient data to generate statistically defensible academic conclusions takes time. And by the time we get around to studying it, a phenomenon is often ubiquitous. This creates a disconnect between academic pursuits and current managerial needs.

Because academics rarely speak to the immediate needs of executives, managers look elsewhere. It has been said that, secretly everyone wants to be led. Practitioners are no different. They are looking for actionable guidance to deal with the serious problems they face now. This leaves them vulnerable to unsound advice or uncertainty about where they can find the advice they need. Today, anyone with an iPhone can broadcast their pontifications online, leading to a plethora of bad information and "fake news." The internet is filled with management fads, get-rich-quick schemes, and short-termism. One study determined that social-media influencers in health and wellness get their messages wrong nearly 90% of the time.

Hence, the final assertion:

3. *Academics like you are in a privileged position to respond to practitioner needs.*
Your background, training, and experience mean you already possess a wealth of expertise in your field. You have been steeped in rigorous analysis.

Introduction

You understand research methods and their uncertainties. You have the foundational skills to deliver solutions to the modern challenges facing businesses and society. And unlike the talking heads out there, academics bring a level of rigor and integrity to their work that other online influencers don't.

If these assertions ring true for you, you are in the right place. By implementing the strategies and tactics discussed in this book, you can respond to executive needs and, by doing so, establish yourself as a respected authority in your field.

Addressing Skepticism Early

Some of you will read the above and disagree. That's normal. This book is not for everyone. You may feel focusing on practitioner-centered work dilutes academic rigor and your professional academic "purpose." This is a common concern. There is a long-standing debate over the relevance of practitioner-centered work versus the rigor and value of traditional academic research (see p. xvii). Some of our academic colleagues look askance at "gurus" and academic thought-leaders. One professor described it as "mere journalism." Another, as "outright activism." Some of the interviewees attributed criticism to frustration on the part of some professors who have not been able to crack the code and break into high-profile practitioner outlets.

While some criticism and confusion about this work is understandable, I and the academic authorities interviewed for this project have found that, when done correctly, this type of work can combine rigor with relevance in ways that positively impact practice in the practitioner's world. (Keep assertions #1 and #2 in mind, and if you are still reading here, these assertions have hit the mark for you.) Success, however, is rooted in a commitment to developing skills and perspectives that stretch the traditional academic tool kit, building upon your background, expertise, and experience. Acquiring these abilities takes time and effort. For those who succeed, the work can be richly rewarding in ways that matter.

Compensation as a Consequence of Value Creation

Another frequent concern is the money academic authorities can command. It's no secret that certain high-profile faculty receive astonishing compensation for their expertise. Some of our colleagues find this unseemly. While academic authorities are often highly paid, in my experience, compensation is a consequence of value creation. Thought leaders are paid only if and when they deliver guidance that improves the lives of managers and their organizations—or, put another way, increases the underlying value of the business. Guidance that can simplify complex challenges and systematize a solution is invaluable in our rapidly changing world. Consequently, some of the value authorities create—in most instances, a mere fraction—can be captured by the academic authority.

For most of the authorities I interviewed, money is not the main motivator. However, many recognized that the additional compensations can help with important life goals like retirement, education for children, and healthcare for loved ones. Not every reader will be interested in this aspect of thought leadership, but I have included an additional section of the book looking at authority value capture. It's an optional part that provides insights for those of you curious about how you can materially benefit from a newfound authority status.

Expanding Your Opportunities

No matter your perspective on practitioner work, one fact is certain: Now is a propitious time for professors looking to expand their skill set and influence to impact the world in positive ways. The VUCA world isn't limited to business. Higher education is also in the midst of its own technological, social, and demographic shifts. Recent headlines include disruption related to:

- **Funding**—Declining government support and increased competition for private gifts and from non-traditional providers are making investment in long-term initiatives and faculty uncertain.

Introduction

- **Demographics**—Demographic shifts and changing attitudes toward higher education create an unpredictable landscape, with declining enrollment impacting demand for qualified faculty.

- **Regulation**—Increased political interference and changes in accreditation, financial aid, taxing endowments, and expectations around student outcomes all pose challenges. Accountability in business education is also rising, with the public and accrediting bodies scrutinizing teaching methods and the impact of research.

- **Legitimacy**—Questions about the societal value of academic pursuits and the applicability of traditional curricula are impugning the relevance of higher education.

- **Technology**—Artificial Intelligence is altering access to actionable information, the way students learn, how faculty teach, and how researchers pursue investigations.

Despite these and many other uncertainties, things could be worse. The outlook for business faculty is better than for our colleagues in, say, the humanities. But the pastures aren't as green as they once were. Budget constraints at many institutions have led to a reliance on contingent, adjunct faculty, who receive lower pay and little job security. For the remaining full-time faculty positions, there is increasing competition, with highly qualified candidates vying for a limited number of positions. And even for established faculty, there is a shrinking upside, with salary increases often limited to cost-of-living adjustments that struggle to keep pace with inflation.

There is also an emergent backlash against an academic touchstone: *tenure*. Once the golden ring of an academic career, tenure is increasingly being questioned. Critics cite cost and lack of flexibility, accountability, and diversity as fundamental reasons to overturn this centuries-old institution. Politicians in a growing number of U.S. states, including Texas, Florida, North Dakota, Louisiana, Iowa, and North Carolina, have introduced legislation or policy changes that would restrict or eliminate tenure. While these initiatives have yet to succeed, the future of lifelong academic employment is in question.

The beautiful thing about establishing yourself as an academic authority is that you can step outside these limits and expand your options. By successfully establishing yourself as a thought leader, you grow your professional circle and open opportunities to experience new organizations and cultures while potentially diversifying your sources of income. In effect, you can create your own economy, uncorrelated with the challenges facing higher-ed. And you can do so while maintaining, or even enhancing, your academic profile and role as a valued member of the faculty. If you have ever considered this a possibility, now is an ideal time—an historic opportunity, really—to step out and establish yourself as a sought-after authority in your chosen field.

What to Expect

First, in Chapter One, "A Tree Hugger in the Halls of Capitalism," I will share my story—not because it is inherently interesting, but so you can see where I come from. I am the least likely guru. You can skip the chapter if you want to get right to the strategies, but I recommend having patience. You do not want to replicate my experience, and this book is your guide to avoiding my errors. I have made the mistakes that allow you to shorten your learning curve dramatically.

The following chapters will then cover the foundational steps you need to take to establish yourself as an authority. They lay out the elements of a development trajectory that can compound over time to build your reputation in your community. Here "community" can take many forms—it might be local, centered around your university or nearby industries, or it could be global, spanning different sectors, geographies, and professional networks; ultimately, it is the audience you cultivate through your work. At the heart of this cultivation process is the Authority Framework, the basic steps you'll execute to establish yourself as an authority. These are the steps that you will engage in over and over again to build your reputation and develop value-added solutions to your audience's challenges.

Rigor Versus Relevance

There is an ongoing debate over "rigor versus relevance" in academic management research, with substantial historic roots. The disconnect arguably began in the mid-20th century, with a movement toward more scientific methodologies in management, similar to what existed in more fundamental academic disciplines, like physics. This led to many formalized and tractable theories in fields such as economics, finance, and operations. Scholars began prioritizing research methods in controlled settings or relying on quantitative data that could be statistically investigated. However, the methods were sometimes ill-suited to the dynamic and messy realities of organizational life.

As academics advanced this work, some practitioners and critics began arguing that the field had become detached from the realities of management practice, claiming research was too abstract and lacked practical relevance to managers. By the 1980s and 1990s, a call for greater relevance in management research took hold. The critics argued that management research should address practical problems, offer actionable insights, and contribute to improving management practices. They dubbed the disconnect "the relevance gap," where management research focused on theoretical debates within a discipline while under-valuing the applicability of the work for managers and organizations. Some scholars noted that ignoring a relevance gap would be untenable in other professional fields, like medicine or engineering.

In its evaluation of the relevance gap, the European Foundation for Management Development (EFMD), an association of business schools, identified untapped opportunities for collaboration and knowledge sharing between academics and practitioners. The study recommended collaboration between managers and faculty to develop more relevant and accessible research. It also interestingly found that managers who were more engaged with academic researchers tended to be more successful in their roles. The assertion is that practitioner-focused research and publication is beneficial for both managers and academics, and should be encouraged.

Further Reading:

"Relevance Lost: The rise and fall of management accounting," by H. Thomas Johnson and Robert S. Kaplan, published in the *Harvard Business Review*, 1987.

"On the Folly of Rewarding A, while Hoping for B," by Steven Kerr, published in the *Academy of Management Journal*, 1975.

"What Makes Research Relevant to Management Practice?" by Denise M. Rousseau, published in the *Academy of Management Executive*, 2006.

"Bridging the Academic-Practice Gap: An exploratory study of the effectiveness of business school interventions," by Karen Niven, Isla Kapasi, and Paul A. Tiffin, published in the *Journal of Business Research*, 2020.

"Incorporating Practical Relevance in Management Research: Conceptualization, measurement, and implications," by Christiane Prange and Daniel R. Denison, published in the *Journal of Management*, 2020.

"Why Practice-Based Research Is Critical to the Future of Management Education," by Trish Reay and Chris Clearfield, published in the *Academy of Management Learning & Education*, 2021.

"The Academic-Practice Divide in Management Education: A call for a renewed emphasis on practice," by Andrea Whittle and David M. Wasieleski, published in the *Journal of Management Education*, 2022.

We'll also cover the touchy subject of compensation. As discussed, this is not required reading if you are not interested in this aspect. However, as an academic authority, you are creating value for your audiences, and compensation can logically follow. I have advice for how to do this elegantly.

I intend for this book to show you how to compress your learning curve, which, for some, can take a decade or more, into months. By following the strategies and tactics discussed in this book, you can enhance and broaden

Introduction

the reach of your professional reputation, build your personal brand, and establish yourself as an authority in your field.

Becoming a thought leader is a journey, not a destination. It requires ongoing learning and development, as well as a commitment to creating valuable content and engaging with your audiences. But with persistence and dedication, you can achieve your goal of becoming a sought-after and highly respected thought leader, making a lasting impact in your field and building a personal legacy for yourself and the ones you love.

• • •

PART I

The Foundations of Authority

CHAPTER 1

A Tree Hugger in the Halls of Capitalism

"Life begins at the end of your comfort zone."
—Neale Donald Walsch

It was the start of winter term at Harvard Business School, and I was bundled up against the frigid Massachusetts cold. I was part of a tiny population of non-Harvard students that had been allowed to register for HBS classes. Finding a chair in Aldrich Hall auditorium, I watched as the HBS students filed in. They wore short-sleeved polos, and some were in skirts. They were obviously denizens of this place, with no need to make the midwinter Charles River crossing like I had.

That's when impostor syndrome hit. What was I thinking? What was a Californian tree hugger like me doing in the hallowed halls of capitalism?

That's where this story begins, with me as a business-school outsider—an environmentalist by sentiment, raised to be wary of capitalists. It's how I grew up. But I am now on the inside, having served and taught at some of the world's top schools, including the Olin School at Washington University, Columbia University, Thunderbird School of Global Management, IE Business School in Madrid, INCAE Business School in Costa Rica, EGADE Business School at

Tech de Monterey, and the Rotterdam School of Management, among others. Impostor syndrome still haunts me. I am not a management scholar, but I have been able to publish repeatedly in top practitioner publications, establishing myself as an academic authority in the field of sustainable business practices.

My beginning at HBS was not auspicious. I wore a ponytail, which stood out among the coiffed high-potential managers populating the Harvard classrooms. When I spoke to the professor during the class break, he said he liked having a few of "my types" in the class because it gave the HBS students an opportunity to see how other people thought. After that, I got a haircut.

I was pursuing a doctorate in International Environmental and Technology Management at the Fletcher School of Law and Diplomacy, which was founded in 1933 as a partnership between Tufts and Harvard Universities. That historic relationship meant I could take nearly half of my course work at Harvard, which is what landed me at HBS. Later, after receiving my PhD, through a twist of fate I landed a job at Madrid's IE Business School, a top-ranked institute where the case method dominated. The school had its own case-publication operation and deep ties with the business community. That gave me an entrée to executives and managers working in the emerging field of business sustainability. I started writing cases based on what I was learning from these managers and began teaching them in my sustainability elective courses. I also found myself assigning Harvard Business Review articles in my courses. When I prescribed more academic articles to the MBAs, they inevitably fell flat. But the students loved the practicality and utility, as well as the timeliness, of the *Harvard Business Review* and *MIT Sloan Management Review* articles.

The Pecking Order

I quickly noticed a pecking order among the faculty. Junior faculty always began in the MBA classroom. If they showed some teaching chops, they were given a shot with the Executive MBAs. But the top of the hierarchy was reserved for the Executive Education faculty. These elite professors gained access to the most-seasoned executives and world-class organizations. And they were handsomely compensated for their skill, in some cases more than doubling their substantial base salaries through exed teaching.

Among these elites, one professor stood out for not only assigning his own cases but also assigning his own Harvard Business Review article, something that would inevitably impress even jaded executives. He was an academic celebrity, invited to speak at leading confabs and business conferences around the world. To me, it looked like nice work if you could get it. So, I began connecting with the school's senior exed faculty, asking if I could observe their teaching and learn something about what they do.

I found there wasn't much of a culture of mentorship in exed. In fact, behind the scenes, faculty would battle to defend their teaching sessions and their additional compensation. Once, I casually inquired about sitting in on a highly regarded professor's executive session, thinking it would be an opportunity to see a professional in action and maybe get some mentoring. The faculty member politely declined, and later I was warned by a colleague that I had "stepped on sacred turf" and had stuck my nose in the wrong place. For this professor and others, it was a zero-sum game where competition could prove costly. However, because I was the fringe "sustainability guy," for most of the exed faculty, I wasn't seen as a threat. Ultimately, several professors graciously let me observe their teaching and even gave me some pointers that improved my classroom performance.

My Aha Moment

Since I hadn't studied in a school of management and did not have an MBA, I didn't really understand the teaching expectations of a professional business school. Initially, I clung to the academic conventions I saw in grad school, loading students with dense readings and long-winded lecturing explanations. It wasn't connecting, something that became painfully clear when I was invited to speak to business professionals visiting our school. I rolled out my academic slides and began pontificating as usual only to have one executive flat out tell me, "We don't have time for theory—do you have anything we can use?" That hit me hard and forced me to rethink my approach.

So, in my MBA sustainability electives, I began leading discussions based on the scant sustainability cases available from case libraries. However, I found students would come after class and say, "You know, that case discussion was great, but can't you give us a framework like we get in strategy or marketing?" Clearly, telling them to "balance the triple bottom line" wasn't getting very far. But no one had created a framework yet. Like my students, I was waiting for someone to produce one that I could use in class. It hadn't dawned on me that maybe I should create one.

As I began writing and teaching my own cases, I was inevitably organizing what I had learned into decision-making frameworks. "How should you think through the issues in this case?" was the question behind every class discussion. Little by little, I started organizing my sustainability courses with my own frameworks, and my MBAs began responding favorably. Students would be able to systematically analyze a case and draw clear, actionable conclusions, something they valued tremendously.

However, the real encouragement came when I began sharing my frameworks with executives. Because I was writing field cases, based on interviews with executives and visits to their facilities, I was building a network of contacts I could reach out to. As I worked on my frameworks, I would sometimes reach out to my contacts and ask about the managerial validity of what I wanted to teach my students. In these exchanges, I began to hear things like, "Yes, that's what's happening. It's interesting that no one had ever spelled it out like that but, yeah, that's what you should be teaching your students. Our managers need to understand this."

That is when a light went on for me. I realized that executives were usually so immersed in resolving the crisis of the moment that they couldn't take the time to reflect on what they were doing. And they usually never bothered to articulate their solutions in a way that could be used to train other managers to replicate their successes. By having the time and interest to investigate what they were doing, I could add substantial value by simplifying and systematizing the solutions to their pressing problems. While I recognized that this was not traditional academic practice—with extensive literature reviews, falsifiable hypotheses, statistically valid sample sets, and detailed data analysis—my work responded to emergent managerial problems for which there was not a lot of available data (in the traditional sense) but a pressing need to make grounded decisions in the face of uncertainty. My research wouldn't get published in an academic journal, but it did fulfill a practitioner need.

At the same time, I saw that most of my academic colleagues weren't doing this kind of thing. In fact, when I told a few that I was working on an article that I hoped to pitch to *HBR* or *MIT Sloan Management Review*, I got some side-eye. "Oh, you can publish that stuff if you want," I was told, "but it's not going to count for tenure." And then, menacingly, "In fact, it'll probably count against you." To be clear, the warnings from my senior faculty colleagues were intended to shield me from the career risks of a practitioner-oriented approach, which did not count when it came time for my tenure review. But I didn't feel like practitioner work and my academic publishing had to be mutually exclusive.

What was frustrating for me and the managers I was engaging with was that faculty research was driven by the concerns of the discipline, not necessarily the needs of managers. I remember one university meeting when this became crystal clear. One of our school's donors had organized a get-together with our top research faculty. The patron, a leading businessperson, suggested that our researchers meet with some of his company's executives and managers. The response from one of my colleagues, who'd published repeatedly in the Academy of Management journals, stunned the executive. "That's a good idea," he earnestly said. "Maybe we can see if our theories work in real life."

Despite my initial lack of experience in publishing in top management journals, I decided to try to pitch my ideas in the *Harvard Business Review*. My search for guidance on how to break in yielded little more than basic submission information on the *HBR* website. Most of the *HBR* authors I had heard of were renowned professors from Harvard Business School, making it seem like an exclusive club accessible only to those with insider connections. Without anyone to coach me, I decided to deconstruct some *HBR* articles to discover any consistent style and structure, choosing articles that resonated with me out of the list of the McKinsey Award winners. After weeks of work and several iterations, I produced what I thought was a good submission.

Despite the apparent barriers to entry, I submitted my work through the standard channels. Then I waited. And then I waited some more. After an agonizing six-month period, I received a brief rejection letter. "Thank you for your article . . . we receive thousands of submissions each year . . . after careful review, we have decided that it does not align with our current editorial needs . . . we appreciate your interest in publishing with us." The rejection obviously stung, but the only feedback was that it didn't "align with their needs." That left me with nothing to build on. When an academic article is rejected, you are given extensive guidance on where you fell short. But, in this world, you get almost nothing.

For a moment, I wondered if I should even keep trying. Maybe I wasn't cut out for the practitioner world. But then I realized that if Thomas Edison had given up after his first failure to create a working light bulb, we might still be in the dark. So, I took this setback the way Edison took his many failures: I had discovered a new way *not* to get published in *HBR*.

I persisted and eventually got a lucky break. Through a series of coincidences, I was able to get the email of a *Harvard Business Review* Press book editor. I found, once I had made contact and established my credibility, that the editor was quite welcoming. That led to ongoing discussion and, making a long story short, an eventual book contract with *Harvard Business Review* Press for my book *Earth, Inc.: Using Nature's Rules to Build Sustainable Profits*. That became the turning point in my high-impact journal publishing.

Leveraging this experience, I began to publish multiple articles in the *Harvard Business Review* and the *MIT Sloan Management Review*. My pieces also found a home in columns for *Forbes* and *Huffington Post*, and I was eventually made sustainability guest editor for the *MIT Sloan Management Review*.

At this point, I was largely self-taught, piecing together the rules of the practitioner publishing game and learning how to communicate effectively with executives. But there were times when I still doubted myself, wondering if I really knew what I was doing or if I was just pretending to fit in.

Impostor syndrome crept in more often than I'd like to admit. But in 2020, everything changed.

Conversations with the Gurus

For decades *Harvard Business Review*, *Sloan Management Review*, *California Management Review*, and the like dominated the practitioner space. This domination had implications for academics. Of the 200,000 business-school professors worldwide, only a tiny percentage ever got the opportunity to publish in these journals. And in a world of more than 20 million executive readers needing their insights, there was untapped potential.

In 2019, a group of academics decided to launch a new publication, *Management and Business Review* (*MBR*), a journal sponsored by eleven business schools as a new platform to share their latest findings and insights with executives around the world. *MBR* was created by academics to assist academics in reaching managers. The goal was to broaden the channels available and bridge the gaps between practice, education, and research. Its articles were aimed at a managerial audience and would both inform *and* inspire action.

In 2020, I received an email from the *MBR* Editor-in-Chief asking me to serve as an adviser. The message was a revelation and felt like vindication. Top schools and leading scholars were championing the practitioner work I had been pursuing for so long. I no longer felt like an outsider—I was being invited to a prestigious group forging new ground in academia. Who knew? Maybe this was the forefront of a larger movement.

The invitation was both an honor and humbling. The editorial board was filled with illustrious names—top-tier professors and senior executives from across the globe. As I read the names of the editors, I recognized *MBR* had brought together the elite. The collective knowledge would be invaluable. What was I going to contribute?

After some thought, I proposed an idea to *MBR*. What if I interviewed our academic colleagues who had cracked the code and repeatedly published in outlets like *Harvard Business Review*? This might allow me to discover some common themes that would help other academics who wanted to write for *MBR*. We agreed it was a good idea, and I started reaching out to our peers.

The interviews with the gurus were stimulating and fascinating. It was a joy to speak with some of the leading academic thought leaders working today and hear their stories. And, indeed, some common themes emerged.

First, for the most part, the authorities had figured things out on their own. They had no guides, roadmaps, or mentors to point the way, something that resonated with my experience as well. Many were lucky to be in schools with executive-education programs and ties to managers. Others had been case writers or had professional managerial experience prior to their doctoral work. While a few were lucky to have an experienced colleague or dissertation adviser they could turn to with questions, most had learned their craft and built their success through the school of hard knocks and persistence.

Next, I found what motivated them was an authentic curiosity and love of the work. Their relevant expertise was founded on their academic preparation but was built by deep immersion in current managerial realities. They enjoyed the engagement process, including the social interaction that came from developing relationships with executives. And they loved the variety and novelty of the work. Again, this resonated with my journey as well. Many described a sense of adventure and discovery that occurred when a light went on and an elusive solution began revealing itself. Others gained satisfaction watching the executives they had met grow and succeed through their managerial careers.

Furthermore, they all described similar approaches and workflows, which also resonated with my own experience. They immersed themselves in the day-to-day world of managers. They cultivated working relationships with managers who could reflect on their work and develop a big-picture perspective. They learned how to identify problems that, if solved, could lead to breakthroughs in performance and impact. And they developed the craft of writing for practitioner audiences in a way that translated technical academic ideas into understandable and compelling messages.

But perhaps most astonishing was this: No one had ever really asked them how they did it. So, I distilled what I learned, integrating it with my own experience, and published an *MBR* article entitled "The Virtuous Cycle of Practitioner-Based Research: How Academics Continually Break New Ground in Management." The article got some attention, and I started getting inquiries from colleagues in different parts of the globe wanting to learn more about the world of academic-thought leadership. That is what motivated me to write this book. I don't pretend to have all the answers, but I have learned a good deal over the last two decades that could dramatically accelerate someone's learning curve.

There is a larger motivation for me. I have met many academics who have powerful insights that I know would help executives do their jobs better and improve organizational performance. Unfortunately, these academics' great ideas go unnoticed, which is especially problematic as we push further into the troublesome 21st century. The world needs thought leaders who can navigate the complex challenges facing businesses today and provide actionable guidance on issues like economic dislocations, digital transformation, supply-chain resilience, diversity and inclusion, ethical AI use, geopolitical risk, and the future of work in a rapidly changing global economy.

I believe academics like us are in a unique position to serve as these experts. This book is my attempt to help you engage executives and deliver compelling solutions that command attention. By doing so, you can position yourself as a sought-after authority in your field—and potentially make a positive impact on a confusing world.

This book isn't just about my journey—it's about helping you shape yours. As academics, we have a unique opportunity to share our expertise in ways that can profoundly impact real-world problems. If you feel the same, then I look forward to accompanying you as we progress through the coming chapters.

• • •

CHAPTER 2

The Authority Motivations and Lifestyle

"The greatest use of a life is to spend it on something that will outlast it."
—William James

At the heart of academic authority is the desire to engage with practitioners and see our work make a difference in the real world. Many of us enter academia with a passion for ideas, research, and teaching, but over time, a deeper ambition emerges—not just to produce knowledge, but to use it to shape the way professionals think and act. There is a desire to build a reputation as someone whose insights are recognized, respected, and actively sought out by professionals in their field. There is an innate satisfaction in seeing your ideas influence real-world decision-making, whether in boardrooms, executive-training programs, or industry conferences. Pursuing authority serves as a way to leave a lasting legacy, ensuring that contributions continue to shape business thinking for years to come.

This chapter explores some of the motivations behind becoming an academic authority, the professional rewards that come with engaging practitioners, and the unique lifestyle and opportunities that arise from this work.

ACADEMIC AUTHORITY

Those Who Have Gone Before

We all know the celebrity management gurus. These thought leaders—often from prestigious schools like Harvard and Wharton—have cracked the code that allows them to craft their message and get it in front of the business leaders who need it most.

Of course, Harvard Business School is known for its exceptional faculty, many of whom are thought leaders in their respective fields. These standout HBS professors include:

Michael Porter: Known for his Five Forces Framework and work on competitive strategy, Porter is perhaps the most successful business-school authority. He established his influential perspective in a series of *Harvard Business Review* articles. Today his strategy frameworks are taught to practically every MBA on the planet.

Clayton Christensen: The late Clay Christensen established his authority in the mid-1990s through *The Innovator's Dilemma*, a book that introduced the concept of disruptive innovation to managers. Despite his passing in 2020, his ideas continue to impact the business world and shape the way executives think about innovation and growth.

Rosabeth Moss Kanter: Her 1979 book, *The Change Masters*, became an international bestseller and established Kanter as a leading authority in the field of organizational behavior. Her ability to translate her academic work into practical insights for managers led her to be named one of the "50 most powerful women in the world" by *Forbes* magazine. She also received recognition from her academic peers with a Lifetime Achievement Award from the Academy of Management.

The demand for these Harvard celebrities is impressive, as I discovered when a European B-school I was working for tried to invite Michael Porter as a keynote for a major event. The story was that Porter's agent told the school that, because we were a business school, he would waive the $125,000 speaking fee if we would simply provide a private jet and luxury suites for him and his team. Upon hearing the news, our school changed tracks and invited Rosabeth Moss Kanter instead. She humbly flew first class.

Our vice deans argued about who would receive her at the airport. The school arranged private guided tours of the national museums for Kanter (accompanied by our vice deans). She reportedly received $40,000 for her 50-minute address. She subsequently took in a tour of the country before returning to Boston and her duties at HBS. While the actual details of the trip may have varied from the story we were told, this was another one of those moments when I thought, *Not bad work if you can get it.*

Some of you might be thinking, "These names are tied to elite institutions like Harvard —places with built-in advantages that can't be replicated elsewhere." However, while the Harvard brand is imposing, academic authorities can be found in many other schools. For example:

Vijay Govindarajan: As the Coxe Distinguished Professor at the Tuck School of Business, Dr. Govindarajan was recognized as one of the world's top business thinkers by Thinkers50 for his work on innovation and strategy and his multiple books, including *Reverse Innovation* and *The Three-Box Solution*. His success didn't come from his affiliation alone; it came from his ability to frame big ideas in ways that business leaders could immediately apply.

Adam Grant: Wharton's Adam Grant is a modern authority with his bestselling books *Give and Take* and *Originals* and a popular podcast. He has been recognized as one of the "world's 25 most influential management thinkers."

Angela Duckworth: Grant's colleague Angela Duckworth established herself as an authority through her work on grit and perseverance, including her book *Grit: The Power of Passion and Perseverance*. She regularly speaks at leading conferences and events.

Again, you may say these thought-leader professors may not be from Harvard, but they are from top Ivy League business schools. They have an unfair advantage. That may be true, but it takes more than an Ivy affiliation to become an authority. These faculty developed a unique set of skills that allowed them to strategically engage with, and respond to, the pressing concerns of today's managers. While I believe that this level of influence is available to any academic willing to learn the ropes and dedicate the effort needed to establish themselves, it is true that a premier academic affiliation provides a boost.

But you don't have to become a celebrity to build an influential and rewarding career as an academic authority. There are many more opportunities out there than most academics are aware of. Academics like you and I occupy a plethora of authority niches. These authorities may speak to smaller audiences, but they are communities that are equally in need of solutions. I have met many of our peers, names you probably have never heard of, who have established themselves as the go-to authority in a specific sub-sector or niche. For example:

Joseph L. Cavinato: The late Joe Cavinato established himself as a leader in the world of supply-chain management, building a massive network of managerial contacts that allowed him to stay on the cutting edge of a field that was rapidly evolving and globalizing through the 1980s, '90s, and the aughts. While not a household name, he became a go-to expert in his field. The Institute of Supply Chain Management even funded an endowed chair for Cavinato that he held until his passing. The ISM ultimately awarded him the J. Shipman Gold Medal Award in 2012 for his distinguished service and contributions to the supply profession. Cavinato is still remembered by his community for his persistence, unselfishness, and ability to inspire a spirit of innovation and giving back to the profession.

Tara Brabazon: Brabazon, a professor at Flinders University in Australia, is a thought leader in the field of media studies and regularly speaks at industry conferences and events. She is a recognized authority in her niche on leadership and innovation in higher education.

Mary Wisnom: An academic thought leader in the field of spa and wellness management, Wisnom hails from Bowling Green State University. She became an authority in a niche many might overlook. Her expertise in amenity management and wellness facilities led to her being recognized with the International Spa Association ISPA Dedicated Contributor Award in 2017. She has also co-authored the industry's definitive textbook, *Spa Management: An Introduction*, ensuring that her insights are being taught in management programs worldwide.

Toby Stuart: A professor at the Haas School of Business at UC Berkeley, Stuart is a recognized authority in a critical niche—technology in healthcare. His expertise allowed him to influence how startups and established companies navigate the commercialization of new medical technologies, showing how targeted expertise can drive real impact.

The reality is that there are many, many opportunities for an academic like you to establish yourself as an authority. Expert opportunities lie in every field, subfield, and niche. Anywhere there is a community of managers confronting challenges of the modern marketplace, expertise is needed. In customer experience, data analytics, sustainability, neuroeconomics, family business, risk management, business continuity planning, ethics: You name it; there is an opportunity. And success is not based on some innate ability or personality characteristics. It is ultimately a question of developing the interest and motivation needed to build an authority position within your chosen professional community.

So, what drives academic authorities? I have found the motivations are varied but basically fall into two big categories: the Professional and the Personal.

ACADEMIC AUTHORITY

The Authority Motivations—the Professional

Most academic authorities I interviewed made the obvious point that business schools are intended to be professional schools. And as in the fields of medicine, law, pharmacy, and social work, professional schools are founded to serve practice.

"There's a certain logic that people at business schools should help businesses to perform and manage better," Andrew Campbell, the Director of Ashridge Strategic Management Centre at Hult International Business School, told me. Doing so requires engagement with the day-to-day realities of practitioners. Medical-school faculty, for example, spend time in hospitals, working directly with patients and interns. But there is a disconnect with business schools. As Ann Majchrzak, Professor Emeritus of Data Sciences and Operations at USC Marshall School of Business, observed: "The difference between managerial professionals and other professions? They actually engage with their community." Unfortunately, business schools turned away from the professional-school model, shifting from addressing the needs of practicing managers to the theoretical needs of academics in disciplinary silos. Today's business schools operate more like graduate schools, serving the interests of academics and their disciplines.

It hasn't always been this way. Harvard Business School was founded in 1908 and was one of the first institutions to offer an MBA. In the 1920s, it pioneered case teaching as an alternative to the traditional lecture-based approach. The case method was introduced to bring the real world into the classroom. By encouraging students to debate and resolve complex, real-world scenarios, it helped develop the judgment needed to navigate uncertainty, something managers face every day. It also allowed students to deal with the fact that disciplinary lenses can produce different solution recommendations.

Take, for example, the case of a company facing declining sales of a flagship product. If you ask a marketing professor, she might diagnose the situation as outdated brand messaging and suggest a new advertising campaign. In contrast, a finance professor might focus on the product's pricing and cost structure, and recommend price adjustments or cost reductions. Operations faculty, in turn, might recommend process optimizations or inventory-management improvements. Human resources? Employee training or team restructuring. And so on. Each discipline, through its unique lens, abstracts a part of the world to analyze and then offers a distinct approach to diagnosing and resolving the same business issue. Case teaching helps address the confines of disciplinary silos. Management in the real world is not achieved through disciplinary science alone. You cannot abstract and control environments in the daily rough and tumble of the free market. A case approach gives students a chance to think across disciplines, integrate different perspectives, and develop the managerial judgment needed to deal with complex, multifaceted real-world problems.

The early practitioner-focused professional school model that allowed this type of teaching eventually gave way to siloed disciplinary science in the 1950s and '60s, driven initially by the influential Ford Foundation and Carnegie Reports criticizing the lack of academic rigor in business education. This prompted business schools to move toward a more theoretical approach, modeled on disciplines like physics, economics, and psychology. As the MBA became standard, faculty hiring shifted toward academics holding PhDs who brought their theoretical-oriented research approaches with them. While these trends enhanced the academic rigor of business-school research, it has also created a growing disconnect between business education and the practical needs of managers and organizations. According to many senior executives, academic research and publishing has ironically become a "vast wasteland" from the point of view of business practitioners the schools were founded to serve.

As the system pressured scholars to publish articles on narrow subjects of interest to other academics, even speaking to non-academics by publishing in the popular media became suspect. As one Oxford professor put it, "Running an opinion editorial to share my views with the public? Sounds like activism to me." Again, it has not always been this way. It has been estimated that, in the 1930s and '40s, twenty percent of articles in the prestigious journals focused on actual practitioner recommendations. Today the share is less than one percent. "While there are exceptions, business-school faculty have become too narrow in the questions they ask, too siloed in their functional areas, and too discipline based," said Vijay Govindarajan, professor at Dartmouth's

Tuck Business School. "We need to create ideas that improve the practice of management. We need rigor and relevance."

Govindarajan points to Louis Pasteur, the renowned French microbiologist, as a model for business academics to emulate. Pasteur's groundbreaking work was characterized by a dual focus: He sought to understand the fundamental scientific principles behind diseases while simultaneously considering the practical implications for improving public health. His research seamlessly bridged theoretical inquiry with real-world application. Govindarajan says this concurrent quest for fundamental scientific understanding and consideration of real-world utility should be the hallmark of business schools.

Warren Bennis and James O'Toole summarized the challenge in an *HBR* article titled "How Business Schools Lost Their Way," writing: "Business-school faculties simply must rediscover the practice of business. We cannot imagine a professor of surgery who has never seen a patient, or a piano teacher who doesn't play the instrument, and yet today's business schools are packed with intelligent, highly skilled faculty with little or no managerial experience. As a result, they can't identify the most important problems facing executives and don't know how to analyze the indirect and long-term implications of complex business decisions. In this way, they shortchange their students and, ultimately, society. Things won't improve until professors see that they have as much responsibility for educating professionals to make practical decisions as they do for advancing the state of scientific knowledge."

While no one is calling on business schools to regress to trade-school status, where faculty dispense war stories, the tide has been gradually shifting. A growing chorus of voices is calling for business schools to demonstrate how they contribute to improving the practice of management and the positive impact it creates in the world. Established organizations like the Association to Advance Collegiate Schools of Business (AACSB) and the European Foundation for Management Development (EFMD) have been promoting a shift toward more relevant research and instruction. And even some government oversight bodies, like the UK government through its Research Excellence Framework, have started to measure the impact of public business schools.

A Turn Toward Relevance

The landscape of business-school research and teaching is undergoing a gradual shift toward greater relevance to practitioners and societal issues. This movement is being driven by academic peer-led organizations and intends to redefine the impact of academic research. The Responsible Research in Business and Management network (RRBM), comprising leading management schools, has played a leading role in framing this transformation, calling on schools and academics to focus on research that addresses critical global challenges. Similarly, the EFMD, with its global reach, has introduced initiatives like the Business School Impact System to assess a school's societal impact through research, teaching, and community engagement.

National and international entities are also advocating for this change. The UK government's Research Excellence Framework evaluates the societal impact of research from public business schools, while the *Financial Times* has launched a ranking system emphasizing business schools' societal contributions. Crucially, the AACSB now requires accredited schools to demonstrate research impact on practice, adding to traditional metrics such as citations and impact factors to include media coverage and practitioner-oriented publication.

Responding to these evolving expectations, many business schools are now producing impact reports, showcasing tangible benefits of their research on society. Schools like Copenhagen Business School, Harvard Business School, INSEAD, and the University of Oxford's Saïd Business School are leading examples, highlighting studies on economic growth, innovation, and social responsibility. These reports not only demonstrate a business school's commitment to relevant research but also reflect a broader trend toward accountability and transparency in the academic world, ensuring that research outcomes resonate beyond the confines of academia and meaningfully contribute to society and business practice.

These trends reinforce the mindset of the academic authorities I interviewed. All of them evidenced a desire to serve practice through their research and publication. Let me be clear: They are all respected academics with impeccable scholarly credentials, but they also have a desire to see their ideas impact the real world, not just the ivory tower. And they recognize the potential influence of having more of their peers adopt similar viewpoints, knowing that engagement with practitioners not only improves the relevance of their research but can also improve the effectiveness of business-school education. As Campbell put it, practitioner work "can inform your teaching much more than highly rigorous research. Undergraduates and MBAs would probably not be interested in reading the typical academic article, but practitioner-oriented publications work well for students."

Think about it. How many *Academy of Management Review* articles have you assigned to your MBA and EMBA students? As Govindarajan says, "I quickly realized I never used anything from my academic articles with my MBAs." This does not mean you abandon academic work. As Richard Ettenson, from Thunderbird School of Global Management, says, "If you're going to be successful at this, you have to be able to play in both worlds. You don't abandon your academic foundations. Your foundations will count, but you've got to learn to articulate your work in a way that's going to have some uptake in the real world."

While not a straight line, the trend toward greater relevance in business-school scholarship is undeniable. One authority I interviewed—Tom Davenport, Distinguished Professor at Babson College—argued that these trends create a window of opportunity for academics like us. Davenport is worth listening to because he has repeatedly pioneered innovative management ideas and has a knack for seeing what's on the horizon. He now sees a transformation of management research underway: "I think we've been on a long swing away from relevance and toward rigor. The pendulum is starting to swing back toward relevance. So, it's a good time to position yourself in this regard." Doing so will put you and your work in better alignment with the higher purpose of the profession we academics are supposed to serve.

Authority Motivations—the Personal

While the professional reasons for becoming an academic authority are important, there are many individual motivations for pursuing this kind of work. Engaging with practitioners allows you to see your work in action, witness its real-world impact, and gain the recognition and respect that comes from influencing key business decisions. By making a tangible impact on business practice and executives, academics open doors to expanded opportunities, recognition, compensation, and an enhanced lifestyle. The authorities I interviewed all indicated that the nature of the work is inherently rewarding and more enjoyable than writing yet another article validating an existing theory. As Campbell explained, there is a sense of exploration and discovery that can be intellectually exhilarating. "It's a little bit like you're an explorer on an expedition," he said. "It feels like that. And it's very exciting." Tom Davenport agreed: "For me, it's been much more stimulating than sitting in my office, writing papers that only a few academics would care about."

The authorities also noted a great sense of satisfaction when their ideas were taken up and applied by managers to enhance their work and organizational performance. As Davenport explained: "The attention to your work can be personally rewarding. Your work is applied and has an impact on the world. It's nice to have an audience." This psychic income is part of the scholars' motivation for making the necessary commitments for successful practitioner work.

On a number of occasions, managers have used my work to improve their organizational performance. In one business conference where I delivered a keynote address, I was surprised to see my framework being flashed on the mainstage by a presenter who then explained how their company had used it to evaluate their product offerings from a sustainability perspective. Seeing my ideas brought to life like that reminded me why this work is so fulfilling. During the presentation, the people I was sitting next to then looked at my name badge and said, "Are you THAT Gregory Unruh?" and pretty soon the news got out that I was actually at the conference. I found people introducing themselves to me at the breaks. The event sponsor approached, beaming, to say how pleased she was that I was at the event. All of this opened new doors to connect with interesting business leaders in ways that advanced my practitioner work, enhanced my status in the professional community, and furthered my understanding of managers' current challenges.

That's another benefit of practitioner engagement: As you become established as a thought leader among your chosen community, you gain great freedom to choose the partners you want to work with. You get to engage with the people you like, find interesting, and who can contribute to your work. You get to choose projects and collaborations that align with your expertise, interests, and values, and can choose the travel and speaking opportunities that excite you and put you in ongoing contact with the very managers you want to engage with. Collaborating on projects aligned with one's expertise, interests, and values offers academic authorities a deep sense of fulfillment. It's not just about the intellectual contribution; it's also about pursuing work that resonates with you on a personal level. This alignment can foster a greater sense of purpose and enthusiasm, contributing to your ongoing professional development and personal well-being.

While engaging with practicing managers as an academic thought leader offers professional growth, it can also offer, as mentioned, financial rewards. Practitioner engagement can be lucrative, but money can be a touchy subject among academics. Many of our peers find it unseemly to consider or discuss the subject. But the reality is that no one will reward you unless you are creating substantial value for them. By learning how to engage with and create solutions to real practitioner problems, you become valuable. And as you deliver value, you can often command substantial compensation. For those of you that are interested in this aspect, Part III will cover the multiple ways authorities can be handsomely and elegantly compensated for their accumulated expertise and insights.

Beyond the monetary rewards, being a thought leader offers you the opportunity to create a lifestyle that aligns with your passions. You gain the freedom to work anywhere and anytime. This is nice because authority status often confers substantial travel opportunities. Joe Cavinato, the supply-chain authority mentioned earlier, would frequently travel with his wife on business-class trips to Europe, Asia, and other destinations as part of speaking and teaching engagements sponsored by companies and associations. While it may seem like a minor thing, business-class travel and accommodations can be a significant benefit. It makes traveling more enjoyable, and you arrive at your destination refreshed and ready to work. And, of course, when the engagement is over, you can take some additional days to explore and immerse yourself in the country you are visiting.

An Authority Lifestyle

Becoming an authority can bring benefits that extend far beyond the traditional boundaries of academia. It allows you to amplify the impact of your work, spreading your insights across various sectors. The status you gain in this role is twofold: You become a recognized figure in your field, and you engage directly with top decision-makers, influencing key strategies and outcomes. Your work becomes a nexus of connection and creation, as you choose projects and partners that align with your values and contribute meaningfully to your field.

As an example of this, in the late 2000s, I had the rewarding opportunity to engage with Intel's Magellan Project in Portugal, an initiative that delivered networked computing to more than 500,000 primary school children. The project not only advanced education but also boosted the economy, creating 1,500 jobs and injecting €2.3 billion into the country's development. Portugal went from the EU country with the lowest internet penetration to one of the leaders. The project was professionally stimulating, and it was energizing to engage with managers and policymakers interested in making a real contribution to their community.

As discussed, becoming an authority can open doors that go far beyond academia. It allows you to amplify your impact, reach new audiences, and build an expanded career on your own terms. The first step is embracing the authority mindset, which I cover in the next chapter.

• • •

CHAPTER 3

The Authority Mindset

*"Intellectuals are rarely successful as leaders.
They are so trapped in their ideals that they cannot venture
out in the real world to win and lead."*
—Awdhesh Singh

For academic thought leadership, mindset plays an important, often undervalued role. The authorities I have interviewed and worked with share a common mindset, which we will explore in this chapter.

As business-school faculty, you are immersed in an academic mindset that values precision, rigor, and the refinement of knowledge. In contrast, the authority mindset goes beyond academia's traditional focus; its goal is to distill knowledge into actionable insights that address today's real-world problems. Beyond the pursuit of knowledge for its own sake, authorities focus on how that knowledge can add immediate value to organizations and their leaders. Authorities are driven by the desire to inform, inspire, and lead change, not just in their field of expertise but also in the wider world. Distinction between these mindsets is important. It's not a question of superiority but rather of purpose and audience. Both mindsets are valuable, but the authority mindset is focused on influencing practitioners and industries, not just furthering academic discourse.

ACADEMIC AUTHORITY

Defining Authority

A useful starting point is agreeing on a definition of what an academic authority is. A typical dictionary definition of an "authority" goes something like this:

> *"An authority is a person with extensive or specialized knowledge about a subject—an expert."*

This traditional view sees an authority as a topic-area specialist, such as "an expert on blockchain" or "an authority on the housing market." It privileges the depth of domain-specific knowledge and aligns well with traditional views of academic proficiency, where authority is derived from mastery of a particular discipline.

Most of you reading this chapter already qualify as an authority by this definition, so, if that was all there was to it, you wouldn't need this book. However, being an expert in a specific topic area doesn't automatically confer authority. We all know many brilliant people who have substantial expertise but no authority. They lack an ability to project their expertise in ways that impact people and their lives.

Thus, while expertise may be a foundation of authority, it's not everything. It is a necessary but insufficient condition of authority.

We need another definition that goes beyond mere expertise:

> *"An authority has the power to influence others, largely through a combination of recognized knowledge about an important topic and a commanding and confident manner."*

This definition gets to the core difference between an academic expert and academic authority. First, you will see that expertise is acknowledged in the definition, but it is conditioned. It is *recognized* knowledge. This is where academics like you have a huge advantage over the many talking heads out there. First, you have an accredited doctoral degree that symbolizes your expertise in a specific field. It signifies to the world that you have made a noteworthy contribution through your original research and advanced skills. It is an endorsement by your peers of your commitment to intellectual rigor and academic integrity. This is powerful in the world of authority and differentiates you among practitioner audiences from the plentiful consultants and talking heads.

Second, as a university professor, you hold a faculty position as a scholar in an institution of higher learning. Your affiliation with a university is a powerful signal among practitioners, giving you a strong foundation as an authority in managerial circles. Despite a general decline in trust in many public institutions, universities still rank highly in public respect, especially compared to business, the media, or government. Richard Ettenson, from Thunderbird School of Global Management, emphasized this point: "The ability university professors have to open doors is remarkable, and it's not available to those without institutional affiliation like us."

Professors are at the pinnacle of the ivory tower and, despite the recent politicization of higher education, public trust in academics is higher than other professions, with more than three-quarters of Pew-surveyed adults having a great deal of confidence that academics act in the public's best interests. Being part of the community of scholars as an academic authority confers substantial prestige, and status, to you. Recognizing, protecting, and leveraging this status is an important foundation of academic authority. Again, by failing to view academia through the eyes of practitioners and the public, most academics I have met undervalue the potential impact of their credentials.

While your credentials are a signal of your expertise and professional values, they are still insufficient for authority. Authority lies beyond expertise and affiliation. It lies in the power to persuade. There is a dynamic interaction with the world, where knowledge is not just possessed but actively applied to shape opinions, drive change, and lead conversations. Authority incorporates the crucial elements of influence and impact, which are pivotal in the realm of academic thought leadership. Most important, authority is applied in service of improving the lives of managers and their businesses.

While academia and thought leadership seek to advance knowledge, they serve different audiences and operate in distinct arenas. They are like two distinct types of games, each with its own playing field and set of rules that condition success and failure.

ACADEMIC AUTHORITY

Playing a Different Game

"Those who can, do; those who can't, teach."
—George Bernard Shaw

While your scholarly credentials are influential and set you apart from internet pundits, if you try playing the academic game with practitioners, it won't work. As an authority, you are playing a different game than as an academic. To succeed, you need to speak to a new, enlarged audience that has not been indoctrinated in the minutiae and jargon of the ivory tower.

As academics, our primary focus is on exploring research questions rooted in disciplinary theories. These questions are addressed through rigorous methodologies that typically involve gathering and analyzing large datasets. For example, we might test a hypothesis like "knowledge transfer (KT) positively impacts firm innovation capacity (FIC)" by analyzing a dataset of multinational corporations, looking at their R&D investments, patent filings, and cross-border collaborations. In this case, while the theory of knowledge transfer is well-established in academic circles, the practical applications for managers—such as how to implement effective KT processes in real time—are often secondary considerations. This gap highlights the challenge of translating scholarly research into actionable strategies for business leaders.

Because our methods additionally need populations large enough to generate statistically significant results, it usually means that the phenomenon under investigation is widespread and long-standing. Long-standing concerns usually already have some standard solutions that practitioners rely on, and while there are always opportunities to improve upon common practice, it usually doesn't address the problems currently keeping managers awake at night. As academics, we are cautious in our assertions and express our results in probabilities. Again, this approach does not meet the needs of practitioners. The chart on page 31 summarizes some differences between the realms of scholarship and authority—between academics and thought leaders.

Comparing Academics and Thought Leaders: Methods and Attitudes

Academic work is inherently descriptive. It aims to explain phenomena, build models, and contribute to theoretical discourse. Thought leadership, by contrast, is prescriptive. It's not enough to describe a problem; thought leaders propose solutions that can be acted upon. This leads to differences in tone and communication. Academics hedge their conclusions, emphasizing uncertainty and nuance, while thought leaders project confidence and clarity, providing actionable recommendations practitioners can implement.

Academic

- Description
- Abstractness
- Uncertainty
- Precision
- Professors

Authority

- Prescription
- Concreteness
- Certainty
- Practicality
- Practitioners

The difference between the worlds can be seen clearly in the titles of "professor" and "practitioner." Professors profess. They share received disciplinary knowledge with uninitiated students. On the other hand, the root of the term "practitioner" is "practice." Practitioners need to *do* something. They have production quotas, quarterly goals, key performance indicators, and a host of other outcomes that they are held responsible for. Anyone who can help them achieve their goals faster and better is a valued resource.

By giving practitioners grounded guidance in situations of complexity and bounded certainty, academic authorities provide a valuable service to managers and organizations.

Successful authorities also project certainty, which can be a challenge for academics. For academics, nothing is certain. It can only be significant. If you're asked, "Are you certain?" the appropriate answer is, "No, but there's a statistically significant probability." It can sound unethical or fraudulent to project certainty for an academic, but in most situations, we don't need to hedge so much. We may not know exactly which direction west is, but if we tell people to walk in the direction of the setting sun, we know that we're pointing them in the right direction. Academics make better authorities because we're trained to gauge the validity of our advice and strike the balance between precision and practicality.

The Authority Mindset

As you can see, the authority mindset is distinct from the typical academic. To articulate this, we will use a simple framework that highlights some key elements that are common for most academic thought leaders I have interviewed. This does not refer to the methods they employ but to guiding principles that shape their approach to making an impact beyond academia. Think of these elements as a pyramid, with each layer building upon the one below.

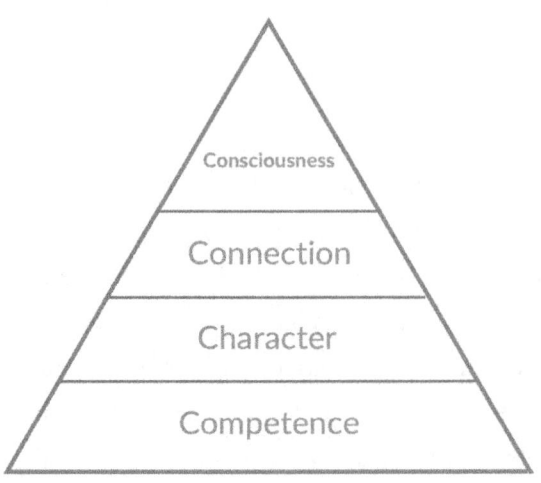

Competence

At the bottom of the mindset pyramid is *competence*, a topic that has already been covered in this chapter. This is the baseline expectation from your audience. They count on you to have the expertise and knowledge necessary to address their challenges. But as we've established, competence alone doesn't make you an authority. The key is moving from simply being an expert to projecting that expertise in ways that influence thinking and action.

Your academic training and critical-thinking skills allow you to analyze and find solutions to emergent challenges. Atop this foundation, you will build your investigations into practitioner concerns and solutions to those concerns.

Character

Building upon competence is the *character* of authority, something that allows a thought leader to translate expertise into authority. The term "character" has two distinct connotations, both of which are important for an authority. One relates to *moral character*, specifically professional commitments and responsibility. The second involves the personality, or *persona*, an authority projects, which impacts their nature and the impression they give. Both are important for authorities.

In an academic context, the character of an individual is largely a question of integrity. Academics maintain the moral and ethical qualities that are expected for scholarly conduct. Integrity signals a commitment to seeking and revealing the truth, something that is pursued in a scholar's research, writing, and communication. Academics are trained to value and protect their intellectual integrity, an attribute that provides great credibility to their work.

I have found practitioners respond with admiration and respect when I make it clear that if I engage in research into a company's challenges, I will reserve the right to say and write what I discover, even if it casts an unfavorable light on managerial decisions.

I was once approached by a European renewable-energy company that had been struggling with increasing competition from Chinese firms. The executive had a clear agenda: He wanted me to write a study claiming that Chinese competition was unfair and to urge the EU to impose stiff tariffs. The problem was, when I dug into the data, it became clear that the facts didn't support the argument. I had to tell him I couldn't write it. He wasn't happy—furious, actually—and left in a huff.

A few months later, I saw a white paper published by a consultant that echoed the executive's flawed argument. The paper came under fire by industry experts and the media, and was quickly buried. Not long after that, I ran into the executive again. He admitted that they had been too eager to blame external forces for the company's challenges. We stay in touch to this day, and I have a credibility with him that was earned through integrity.

In this sense, academic character is about preserving your independence. It requires consistency in maintaining intellectual honesty and objectivity in research and evaluations, regardless of external pressures or incentives. This is important, because, when engaging in the world of for-profit business, financial incentives can be plentiful. Academic authorities must carefully guard their independence in these situations. Unlike consultants being paid to fulfill a client's request, authorities are engaging with practitioners to advance the state of knowledge and enhance practice in the entire community. They are not working for the sole enrichment of a single company or executive. Nor are they working for self-enrichment at the expense of the truth. Preserving the ability to confidently speak truth to power is foundational for an academic authority.

By maintaining this mindset as a core element of one's character, academic authorities foster a reputation of reliability and trustworthiness. A reputation cannot be bought; it must be earned by repeatedly demonstrating and defending your professional character. And, as Benjamin Franklin stated, "It takes many good deeds to build a good reputation, and only one bad one to lose it."

The second connotation of "character" has to do with how someone thinks, behaves, and acts in the world. It is about the *persona* they project to the public. Everyone presents a character to the world—some predominant way they are perceived by an audience. In fact, most people have multiple personas depending upon the situation—the persona of the spouse, the son or daughter, the professor, the parent, and so on. In most cases, these images are an incidental result of our natural personality traits and the exigencies of the situation. They are not a conscious act. In thought leadership, your character needs to be more intentional—more strategic.

One character archetype all faculty tend to unconsciously adopt is that of the "professor." This character embodies a scholarly demeanor and a focus on intellectual discourse. The professor usually appears somewhat reserved, prioritizing the rigor of content over personal connections. Again, we don't necessarily choose this character consciously, but it becomes conditioned after years of training in the halls of academia. A recognizable and attractive character, by itself, is not usually sufficient for projecting authority to practitioner audiences.

As an authority, you can cultivate a set of character traits that make you recognizable and signal your competence and capabilities to an audience. The idea of an authority character has a good deal in common with the idea of a personal brand. Personal branding is the practice of creating and promoting a consistent identity that represents a person's values, skills, experiences, and personality to a specific audience. It's a crafted narrative that defines your character in a way that makes you quickly recognizable to your community, while differentiating you from other authorities in a potentially crowded market.

A character image is a simplified yet powerful tool that encapsulates your complex identity. It is projected, not for comprehensiveness, but as a vehicle to engage and influence others. Its strength lies in its simplicity, making it a compelling and persuasive element that resonates with your audience.

When considering your authority character, it is important to embrace a clear idea of who you are and what you want to project to your audience. As an academic, an almost automatic character is that of the *accessible expert*. This persona emphasizes not just expertise but also the ability to make complex information understandable to the general public. Media outlets and journalists seek out these people because of their ability to communicate complicated issues in ways that are intelligible to lay audiences. Every academic authority should cultivate and communicate the character of the accessible expert to their audiences.

Authority Character Types

Your authority persona serves as a mental signature, allowing others to quickly understand who you are and who you serve. Some personas are specialized, deeply rooted in a particular industry or domain, while others are generalist, offering broad, cross-industry insights that apply in multiple settings. These personas aren't gimmicks but practical ways to distill and communicate your expertise effectively. Here are some examples of each.

Specialized Personas (industry-specific)

These personas focus on a well-defined industry or sector, positioning their expertise within a specific professional domain.

The Leader's Coach—Rooted in leadership and organizational change, this persona helps executives and managers navigate complex challenges. Scholars like John P. Kotter, known for his work on change leadership, and Warren Bennis, a pioneer in leadership studies, exemplify this type.

The Tech Futurist—This authority makes sense of emerging technological shifts, helping leaders anticipate and adapt to disruptive innovation. Stanford's Erik Brynjolfsson, who studies the economics of digital transformation, exemplifies this persona.

The Startup Sage—Focused on entrepreneurship and innovation, this persona guides founders and venture leaders through the complexities of scaling and strategy. Steve Blank, creator of the Lean Startup methodology, embodies this role, influencing both startups and academic programs at Stanford, Columbia, and Berkeley.

The Global Strategist—A trusted advisor for businesses navigating international markets, this persona helps leaders develop strategies for globalization. Pankaj Ghemawat, at IESE Business School, conducts research on cross-border business strategy and is an exemplar of this type.

The Brand Architect—Focused on marketing, brand influence, and consumer behavior, this persona deciphers what makes marketing efforts succeed or fail. Wharton's Jonah Berger, whose work on viral marketing is widely applied in industry, is a strong example.

Generalist Personas (industry-agnostic)

These personas focus on broader, cross-industry insights, making them valuable across different sectors and audiences.

The Simplifier—Complexity overwhelms people, and many practitioners crave clarity. This persona excels at distilling intricate theories into intuitive, actionable insights. As Thunderbird's Richard Ettenson says, "I'm not the smartest guy in the room, but I strive to be the simplest." If your strength lies in cutting through jargon, this may be the right identity for you.

The Systems Thinker—This persona sees connections across industries and disciplines, integrating diverse perspectives into an holistic approach. Instead of focusing on a single field, they synthesize knowledge from multiple domains to uncover patterns and insights.

The Behavioral Strategist—This persona applies psychology and behavioral science to decision-making across industries, helping practitioners understand how people think and act. An academic like Richard Thaler, who brought behavioral economics into business, is a good example.

The Big Idea Person—These authorities develop frameworks that can be applied across multiple industries, helping leaders rethink core assumptions. Thought leaders like Clayton Christensen, who pioneered disruptive innovation theory, exemplify this approach.

Choosing Your Authority Character

Your authority character should align with both your expertise and the audience you intend to cultivate. Whether you focus on a specific industry or adopt a broader perspective, your persona will shape how practitioners perceive and engage with your work. The key is to be intentional. Thought leaders don't leave their positioning to chance—they craft it deliberately to maximize impact.

The examples beginning on page 36 provide some illustrations of authority character types that can undergird your personal-branding efforts. These samples draw from actual academic thought leaders but also tap into more universal archetypes that most people recognize. A character serves as a mental shortcut for people, allowing them to identify and quickly connect with you and your message, while also helping establish credibility and trust. As such, you can tap into your audiences' preconceived notions of characters that exude the characteristics your image is intending to communicate. By making mention of historic, contemporary, and even fictional characters, you can associate your personal brand with their virtues in the minds of your audience. Often your audience will see themselves, or what they aspire to become, in these characters as well.

The power of a consciously chosen persona that aligns with your goals and values comes from communicating it effectively. For instance, if you adopt the character of a Leader's Coach, the term exudes qualities such as effective communication, empathy, inspiring leadership, and the ability to empower others. Your audience will connect these attributes to your professional identity, allowing you to exert influence over how you are perceived and received. Much of the communication can be done indirectly as you deliver valuable insights and content to your audience. However, while your actions and appearance will often speak for themselves, there are times when you might state your chosen image explicitly. This can be especially helpful in media interactions, as it ensures your intended message is clearly conveyed. Consistency in your character helps solidify your personal image, making it an effective tool for quickly building rapport.

The possibility of creating a persona presented itself to me unexpectedly in the early days of my authority trajectory. In the 2000s, a conference planning committee decided they wanted to invite Al Gore to give his iconic *An Inconvenient Truth* speech. His work on climate change had just earned him an Oscar and a Nobel Prize, so they figured he would be the perfect headliner. But when they reached out and got his speaking fee, they were shocked. It was more than $100,000 per appearance. The budget simply couldn't handle it.

The conference chair, clearly frustrated, said, "We need to find a cheap Al Gore!" That's when they reached out to me. I became the "Cheap Al Gore," a persona I adopted with humor and enthusiasm. While I didn't receive anywhere near Gore's fee, the opportunity allowed me to substantially raise my own speaking fees just by association with the persona of the former vice president. It became a turning point in how I presented myself. While I had my own style that resonated with the audience, the association with Al Gore and being the "affordable alternative" allowed me to carve out a new niche. I even published an article titled "The Cheap Al Gore" in my *Forbes* column, something that made great collateral to send to meeting planners when they reached out to me for a keynote presentation.

The Authority Positioning Stack as Part of Your Authority Character

To effectively position yourself as an academic authority, it helps to understand and build your Authority Positioning Stack. This framework consists of three key elements—*Bestowed*, *Borrowed*, and *Built* authority—each of which contributes to shaping your authority profile. (A fourth element, *Bought* authority, depends on having a public-relations budget and is not usually applicable at the beginning of an authority's development, so it won't be covered here.) Think of this stack as a layered foundation that demonstrates not only your expertise but also how you present yourself to the world.

Bestowed Authority

Bestowed authority refers to the status you gain through formal titles and credentials. As an academic, your position (e.g., professor, researcher, or chair) and place of graduation (the institution where you earned your degree) are powerful signals of your expertise. These elements immediately convey credibility because of the traditional respect society holds for academic institutions. Additionally, any honors or awards you've received further enhance this bestowed authority, signaling to the public and peers that your work has been recognized and valued by prestigious bodies.

Your character as an academic authority should always incorporate and emphasize these formal credentials, which most other pundits and talking heads do not have. Bestowed authority sets a firm foundation with practitioner audiences that value the gravitas of institutional affiliation.

Borrowed Authority

Borrowed authority refers to the external validations and associations that can further boost your credibility. These come from the praise you've received from others in the form of testimonials, endorsements, or recognitions. In academic circles, this often comes through publishing in prestigious journals. A journal with a high-impact factor, for example, serves as an indirect indicator of the value of our work. When we publish in these journals, their reputational halo is effectively transferred—or "borrowed"—by us, enhancing our perceived status among our disciplinary peers.

Outside of the ivory tower, praise from respected executives or industry leaders in a public forum can similarly elevate your stature. Press mentions or publication outlets like *Harvard Business Review* or *Forbes* also allow you to borrow their credibility, amplifying your influence and reinforcing your standing as a thought leader. To maximize this Borrowed authority, you must actively cultivate testimonials, endorsements, and recognitions. By strategically seeking opportunities to showcase your work in reputable venues and developing relationships with industry associations, you can systematically build your profile and expand your reach.

Built Authority

The final layer, Built authority, represents the authority you actively develop over time by sharing your experiences, perspectives, and ideas. Unlike Borrowed authority, which relies on indirect validation, Built authority stems from direct recognition of your work's value and impact. In academia, this is most clearly reflected in citation counts, which serve as tangible evidence of your research's utility and influence. While the reputational halo of a prestigious journal is borrowed, citations indicate that others are actively using and building upon your ideas—an acknowledgment of your contributions to the scholarly community.

Your authority character should reflect the unique story of your professional journey, as you build your authority through engagements, publications, speaking engagements, press interviews, and so on. Built authority gives depth to your character, as your unique perspective sets you apart from others in the field by showcasing your distinct voice. As your audience grows, the attention to your work demonstrates the resonance of your ideas. Interestingly, having paying clients powerfully reinforces your authority, proving that your expertise delivers actionable value and is in demand. Over time, these direct measures of impact solidify your authority, establishing you as a trusted voice in your domain.

Together, these three forms of authority—Bestowed, Borrowed, and Built—form your complete Authority Positioning Stack. As you refine your character, you will draw from each of these layers to project an image that resonates with your audience and reinforces your credibility. Your Bestowed credentials provide the foundation; Borrowed authority amplifies your influence through external validation; and Built authority creates a compelling narrative that showcases your unique contributions and leadership in your field.

By consciously shaping your authority character through the lens of the Authority Positioning Stack, you not only enhance your professional persona but also cultivate a strong, lasting influence that positions you as a trusted and respected thought leader.

Connection

Your established character allows you to build on the next mindset level: connection. Your character creates a conceptual shorthand for your audience to facilitate quick connection. Connection is a fundamental part of the authority mindset. You will need connection to build a network of practitioner contacts and ultimately an audience for your ideas.

While it may seem obvious, a distinguishing factor about authorities is that they have an audience. Leaders, by definition, have followers, and to be an authority, you must have followers, that is, an audience for your ideas.

Connecting effectively with this audience is fundamental for establishing yourself as an authority.

While it is clear that authorities need an audience, an important question is: *Why do audiences need authorities? Why do they seek out experts like you?* Whether we like it or not, in novel and uncertain situations, people look for a guide. It's said that, secretly, everyone wants to be led. We don't want to do all the hard thinking for ourselves, so we look for leaders, for thought leaders, who can provide guidance and clarity in unclear situations. In a world brimming with competing information and ideas, people naturally gravitate toward people who can simplify complexity, offer clarity in ambiguity, and provide actionable insights. This is where the role of an academic thought leader becomes pivotal. By offering informed perspectives, thought leaders help their audience navigate challenges, embrace opportunities, and make informed decisions.

The connection you build with your audience will ultimately determine your standing in the community and the influence you can yield. For authorities, an audience is more than just a group of listeners or readers. It is the community in which they immerse themselves and where the thought leader's ideas take shape. An audience provides the information, feedback, and validation that are critical for refining and evolving a thought leader's ideas. This engagement simultaneously enhances the thought leader's influence and deepens their understanding of the needs of their audience. Cultivating an audience is not just about amassing followers; it's about building a community of engaged individuals who are actively interested in your ideas. For an academic thought leader, an audience is both the proving ground and the launchpad for ideas that can impact the world. The relationship is not merely important; it's symbiotic.

Through this engagement, most academic authorities develop a sense of service to the community. It is a natural progression as you engage with practitioners, get to know their aspirations and challenges, and begin to see ways that, through your work, you can help them achieve their goals. Your work is in service of a group of people that you care about and a set of problems that you find intellectually stimulating. For this reason, an important decision every authority needs to make is which community they intend to serve.

You should take time to think carefully about this. It should, of course, take full advantage of your disciplinary expertise, but it should also allow you to express your passions and engage with people you find interesting and enjoyable. Selecting a community isn't just a strategic decision; it's a pathway to fulfillment and impact. When you are genuinely interested in the issues and people of a particular community, your work transcends the boundaries of obligation and becomes a source of inspiration and personal satisfaction.

I often tell people I would be doing this work even if I wasn't paid for it. Of course, I am compensated handsomely for my efforts, but I also find inherent fulfillment in understanding the challenges facing my community, discovering solutions to their problems, and delivering them in ways that enhance their ability to achieve their goals.

For example, I have been fortunate to engage with the Sustainable Brands community and have frequently spoken at their events. It wasn't just the presentations that left an impact, though; it was the midsummer evenings spent around beach bonfires in San Diego, engaging in candid conversations with executives from some of the world's leading companies. These fireside chats became a place to step away from the formalities of the conference and dive into real, raw discussions about the challenges, as well as the aspirations, these leaders faced in driving sustainability initiatives forward. Over time, these informal conversations helped evolve my work. I learned as much from them as they did from me, and, together, we created a shared understanding that could help shape the next round of sustainability practices.

It was in moments like these that I felt connected to the Sustainable Brands community, not just as a speaker but as a collaborator and contributor. Those experiences reminded me of the importance of connection and community in solving the complex issues facing businesses today.

Consciousness

Finally, at the top of the authority mindset pyramid is consciousness. Here we are discussing our individual focus and the level of inclusiveness in our vision and work. Developmental psychologists like Jean Piaget, Erik Erikson, Clare

Graves, and Abraham Maslow explored how human consciousness evolves over our lifetime. Their work has been built upon by Lawrence Kohlberg, Carol Gilligan, and Robert Kegan to identify developmental stages. Here we will simplify their work and identify three developmental stages that have implications for the mindset of an academic authority.

The first level is *egoic*, where the focus of consciousness is self-centered and largely unconcerned with the needs of other people. As we mature, we enter a second *ethnocentric* level, where our identity shifts from the individual to the group or tribe we associate with. This is the time of the teenager wanting to fit in and be part of a clique, adopting the habits, beliefs, and behaviors of a group. Finally, many people evolve beyond an ethnocentric identification and begin to see the similarity and interdependence with every other group. This is often called a *world-centric* level and is characterized by an awareness of global interconnectedness and a desire to contribute to the greater good of everyone, not just the tribe.

The evolution through these levels of consciousness—from egoic to ethnocentric to world centric—is a lifelong journey of expanding awareness and influence. After developing through the levels, while one may become our center of gravity, we continue to access all three levels of consciousness, and all three levels have something to contribute to our authority journey.

Egoic Level of Consciousness: At the egoic level, the focus is on you as an individual. Part of this is your personal development and expertise; the other is your personal success and gain. When focusing on this stage, authorities concentrate on deepening their knowledge and honing a unique voice and perspective. It's a period marked by learning, self-reflection, and personal development. It is also about developing a character that differentiates you from other thought leaders.

At the egoic level, it is also important to understand how you will benefit from the effort you exert in becoming a recognized thought leader. The personal rewards are motivational and an important driver for many authorities. There are obviously ways to gain financially, and these will be discussed in later chapters, but there are also less-tangible benefits. When you become an authority in a community you care about and enjoy, you gain a new level of status and celebrity, and there are perquisites that come with it. You engage with interesting people on intellectually stimulating issues that are consequential for organizations. Your ongoing engagement creates a virtuous cycle of continuous personal growth, recognition, and impact that will motivate you to continue deepening your authority.

Ethnocentric Level of Consciousness: At the ethnocentric level, the focus is on the community and audience you are serving. It is about developing a leadership role in a community and building meaningful relationships with its members. By influencing and shaping the norms, values, and goals of the field, you see yourself within the larger system and develop a growing sense of responsibility. Your work becomes one of service to the community as they apply your ideas, and you celebrate the successes of community members. When they achieve milestones using the strategies you've developed, it not only enhances the credibility of your ideas but also amplifies your reputation as a thought leader. Each success story becomes a shared victory, strengthening your position within the community. As community members champion your ideas in their networks, your reach extends, often leading to invitations to collaborate, speak at events, or contribute to larger projects.

World-centric Level of Consciousness: At the world-centric level, you expand your perspective and influence by recognizing the value and importance of the community within the larger socioeconomic, or even planetary, context. This phase is marked by a focus on how your work and expertise can contribute to helping the community address broader societal and global challenges. There is an awareness of global interconnectedness and a commitment to contributing to the global good. Academic leaders at this level begin establishing themselves as sages and often establish a lasting legacy.

Take, for example, Peter Drucker, recognized as the father of modern management. Drucker focused his early work on disciplinary topics of business management, emphasizing the objectives of a company, the role of a manager, and how corporations could be structured for efficiency. Over time, however, his work evolved. He began exploring how societal trends were influencing organizations and, conversely, how organizations were impacting society.

World-centric Thought Leaders

Michael Porter, much like Peter Drucker, started his career focused on the discipline of business strategy, becoming widely recognized for his work on competitive advantage and the Five Forces Framework. His early work was instrumental in shaping how organizations analyzed their industry environments and structured themselves to gain competitive positioning. Over time, however, his research evolved, and Porter shifted his attention to the broader role that businesses play within society. He began exploring how companies could not only achieve profitability but also contribute to societal progress through strategic corporate social responsibility. In particular, his work on shared value reframed the purpose of businesses, arguing that firms could simultaneously create economic value while addressing social challenges. Just as Drucker had recognized the importance of nonprofits and the responsibilities of corporations to society, Porter, too, led conversations on how businesses could be powerful agents of social change while remaining competitive in the marketplace.

Clayton Christensen, known for his pioneering work on disruptive innovation, initially focused on how small, nimble companies could outmaneuver industry giants through simpler, more-affordable solutions. His early research revolutionized the way businesses understood innovation and competition, emphasizing how disruption could topple even the most established firms. However, as Christensen's career evolved, so did his interests. He expanded his focus beyond the business world to examine how disruptive innovation could be applied to sectors like healthcare and education. Christensen's later work argued that the same principles of disruption that applied to industries could drive significant improvements in society, by making essential services more accessible and affordable.

ACADEMIC AUTHORITY

> Originally focused on topics like organizational behavior and corporate culture, **Rosabeth Moss Kanter**'s early work explored how companies could build more inclusive and empowering environments, particularly through her seminal book *Men and Women of the Corporation*. As her career progressed, Kanter turned her attention to how organizations can become agents of societal change. Kanter's work demonstrates how corporate strategy can be deeply intertwined with social responsibility, creating a new model of leadership that values both economic success and societal impact.

He led conversations on diverse topics like the knowledge worker, nonprofit organizations, and the societal responsibilities of corporations. Drucker's evolving perspective highlighted a world-centric consciousness, understanding that effective management practices were critical for not only business success but also for addressing societal changes.

The transition to the world-centric stage represents a significant expansion of perspective, where the focus of your authority is on creating an impact that transcends geographical and cultural boundaries, aiming for a global positive change and building a lasting legacy from your work. The integration of these stages—from egoic to ethnocentric to world centric—represents a progression from mastering personal expertise to contributing to wider conversation about contributions to society and humanity. These stages offer a road map for one's evolving perspective and approach to leadership, from personal growth to globally inclusive contributions to the world.

Stepping Up to Authority

Here is a little-known secret about becoming an authority. No one is going to announce that you are an authority. Academic authorities I have met simply decided for themselves that they were authorities. They unilaterally took on the mantle of authority and began to think and speak as an authority. Some people will hesitate to make this step. Impostor syndrome will intrude in their thinking, and they will consciously or unconsciously question whether they have what it takes to claim authority status. An antidote to this internal dialogue is to look outward. Look to the community of practitioners you have the potential to serve.

Ask yourself, *Do I think managers can benefit from my expertise?* Again, many people underestimate the value of their expertise. What we think of as common knowledge usually isn't. Do you know things that could help managers do their job better? Are you capable of uncovering better ways for them to achieve their goals?

If so, then there is a second question you should ask yourself: *Do I think I can deliver the expertise better than someone else*? Do you feel like you can craft compelling ways to communicate your expertise that will resonate with practitioners? Remember, one of the biggest challenges for practitioners is that they cannot easily understand the relevance of many useful academic insights because we fail to translate them into actionable frameworks that are intelligible to managers. As such, they often look to less-reputable sources that lack the level of integrity and rigor academics bring to concerns.

Finally, if you believe you can deliver insights, then there is a final question to ask yourself: *If I do not deliver these insights to practitioners who can use them, will they ever get them at all?* If you have valuable insights or the capacity to *discover* valuable insights, that can help managers do their work better. If no one else is providing those insights, then there is an implied responsibility for you to share what you know. By not stepping up as an academic authority, you are doing a disservice to the people your discipline professes to serve.

By stepping into the role of an academic authority, you are not just amplifying your own voice—you are fulfilling a vital need within the business community. There are executives, managers, and decision-makers who are hungry for insights that only you can provide. If you remain silent or keep those insights within the walls of academia, the practical impact of your knowledge diminishes, leaving a void in the world where real problems need real solutions. This isn't just an opportunity; it's arguably a responsibility. By ensuring your work helps those who can benefit, you not only elevate your standing but also create a legacy for the future.

• • •

CHAPTER 4

Authority Development Trajectory

*"The credit belongs to the man who is actually in the arena . . .
who strives valiantly; who errs . . . and who, at the best,
knows in the end the triumph of high achievement."*
—Theodore Roosevelt

While every academic's journey to becoming a thought leader is unique, most follow a generally predictable path. Through my interviews, I have mapped out the route many academics take to becoming an authority in their field. I call it the *Authority Development Trajectory*. Understanding the trajectory will help you know what to expect and also what to look out for during your distinct phases of growth.

There are three phases along the trajectory: an initial *Investment Phase*, a *Liftoff Phase*, and a *Maintenance Phase*. This trajectory follows an S-curve. As with other S-curves, the path begins with a period of slow growth, moves into a period of rapid expansion, and finally plateaus as growth stabilizes at the upper limit.

All the phases are important. My goal with this book is to get you to the Liftoff Phase. Once you get to liftoff, you will find that the effort needed to scale up your influence and impact diminishes, while the opportunities available to you multiply. Upon reaching this point, your attention can turn to building an ongoing authority enterprise atop your authority foundation.

Once you reach the Liftoff Phase of the trajectory, a world of opportunity opens up, allowing you to leverage your status to build a lasting legacy and generate the resources needed to take care of yourself and your loved ones. With today's technology, anyone can create a lean, powerful organization that amplifies your influence. Here you will be scaling your authority into a thriving, sustainable enterprise that ensures both personal and professional fulfillment. All of this becomes possible when you have reached authority liftoff, thus the attention paid to it in this book.

The following sections provide an overview of the trajectory and what to expect in the different phases. I dive deeper into the activities during each phase in subsequent chapters. Here you can see how they fit together as part of your authority evolution.

But first, there is the question about where this trajectory fits within your academic career. The main issue is whether you should engage in practitioner work while you are a tenure-track professor. Most good faculty mentors would recommend focusing on meeting the tenure expectations of your institution before diving into practitioner work. Securing tenure provides the stability and academic credibility needed to fully engage with external audiences without compromising your scholarly commitments. However, I might be an exception here. Coming from a discipline outside of management, I didn't have that traditional guidance. Instead, I pursued my academic research and practitioner work in tandem, allowing each to inform and enrich the other.

Even if your primary focus should be publishing in A-level journals, there's still room to begin engaging with practitioners early on. Universities often provide opportunities—through industry partnerships, conferences, or executive-education programs—that allow you to understand the practitioner perspective without diverting from your research priorities. By thoughtfully integrating these experiences, you can build a foundation that not only strengthens your academic authority but also positions you for broader impact once tenure is secured. Having this book and understanding the development trajectory presented here can provide a road map for you as you advance in your professional career pre-tenure and beyond.

The Investment Phase

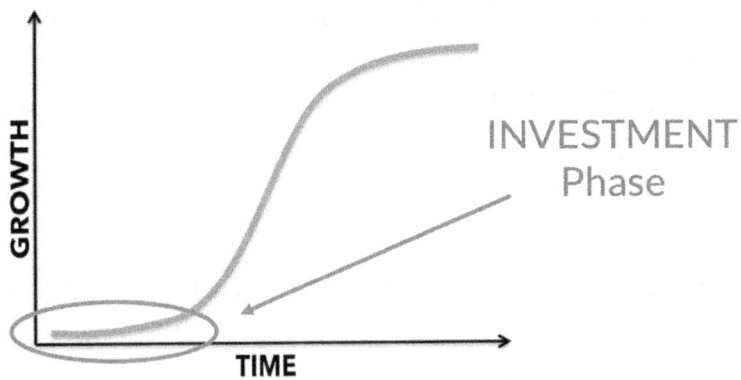

During the Investment Phase, you'll build the foundation upon which your authority status grows. The first part of this phase is largely introspective. You need to first clarify your motivations and goals for pursuing an authority trajectory. What do you want to achieve as an authority? You also clarify the topic area and field you plan to focus on as well as the preferred community of practitioners you plan to engage with. Choose topics and communities that you find inherently interesting, engaging, and rewarding, and your authority work will be far more satisfying and life-enriching.

In this initial phase, you survey the state of knowledge in the field as well as the players operating in the practitioner space. You are probably cognizant of the germane academic literature, if the field is aligned with your disciplinary expertise, but you will also find many non-academic sources that practitioners look to. Executives rely on industry trade books, white papers, and reports instead of journal articles because academics tend to do a poor job translating their findings for managerial use. You will read the top practitioner books on your topic, identify the leading consultancies in your field, and review the content they are producing for clients. You will identify the leading industry associations and see what services they offer for professional members, such as conferences, workshops, training, or certifications. By doing so, you'll begin developing a synthesis of the state of the field that incorporates your unique perspective.

As your synthesis evolves, you'll also start building a network of professionals and contacts. This will include practitioners but should also include other authorities and influencers. You will engage with them through interviews and other interactions, seeking to understand the current conversations and trends in the field. Through this type of networking, you begin establishing yourself as part of the community.

As your knowledge of the community's concerns and issues grows, you can start producing content and pushing it out on an ongoing basis. You have to be careful here and do this efficiently so that you don't fall into the sinkhole of social media.

During my early days, I wasted a lot of time using social-media platforms. Before liftoff, I landed my first book contract with *Harvard Business Review* Press. It was in the 2000s, and social media was on the rise. When I met with the Harvard marketing team, they told me I needed to "build my platform," which meant creating Facebook, LinkedIn, and Twitter accounts and using them to amass followers. For more than a year, I worked to create fresh posts for Facebook and LinkedIn every week and was posting on Twitter several times a day. But when I stepped back to evaluate its effectiveness, I found it had neither contributed appreciatively to sales of the book nor facilitated connections with the practitioners I was hoping to reach. Social media can play a role, but what works for online influencers doesn't necessarily work for academic authorities.

The goal in the Investment Phase is to cultivate an audience of people that want to hear your message. You do this very strategically by creating ongoing impressions of you and your expertise in the community. Among the more efficient approaches I found is to identify where your audience is already congregating and finding ways to insert yourself into the conversations they are already having. We will discuss how to do this in the upcoming chapters.

As you produce valuable content and insights, you begin refining your unique perspective and voice. Your academic character, as discussed in the previous chapter, will begin to take shape, and people will begin recognizing you along these lines. You will also begin to clarify your preferred communication formats for reaching your audience. This could be anything from articles, blog posts, videos, podcasts, and, where appropriate, social-media updates. As you produce content that is useful and valuable to your community, people will begin looking to you for insights, perspectives, and solutions to the problems they are facing, establishing you as an authority within your community.

During this phase, it is important to be patient and persistent. You may feel like you're not getting anywhere initially. In fact, I have found many potential authorities give up at some point during the Investment Phase because they do not feel they are getting the recognition they deserve from their efforts. Thunderbird's Rich Ettenson concurs: "It can be hard work. Much like getting publications accepted into A-level academic journals. It's that level of persistence." But if you stick with it, continue to deepen your understanding of community concerns, and refine your approach, you will reach a tipping point. I call this the Liftoff Phase.

The Liftoff Phase

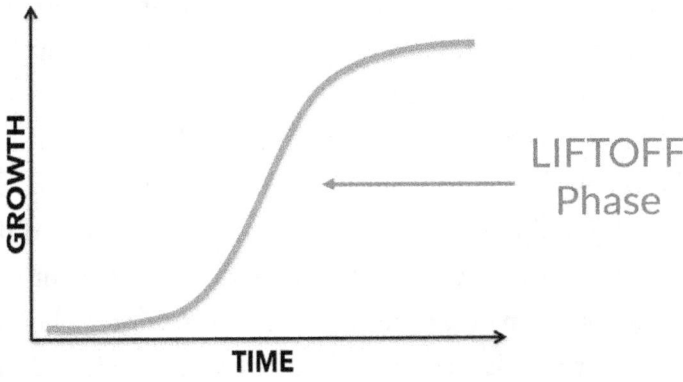

During the Liftoff Phase, you start to see name recognition and build an established reputation within your community. The awareness cultivated during the Investment Phase has people recognizing your unique voice and messaging, sparking interest among a growing fan base.

What makes liftoff possible is that you've created a critical mass of content, impressions, and presence in the community. As you project a consistent perspective and image, your audience begins affiliating with your ideas and message, as well as the character you present as an authority. You deliver solutions that improve organizational performance and help practitioners achieve managerial goals.

The Liftoff Phase moves from the initial awareness to taking action on the thought leader's guidance and wanting to engage directly. The more people hear about you, the more they want to know. Synergies emerge among the different artifacts you've been putting out into the community. Interactions among your different types of presences emerge, and people discover you organically. For example, someone might see your article and then search the web for a webinar you're offering. Or they might see your TED Talk and decide they want to hear you speak in person. People are attracted to your ideas and unique perspective, and begin seeking you out.

At this point, many authorities will have published a book, which is an important authority vehicle. Traditionally, book publishing was seen as a way to establish yourself as an authority. However, I find that a book is a better vehicle for consolidating the Liftoff Phase. The book should be a culmination of the work you have done during the Investment Phase and a place where you can showcase your unique synthesis of the field, the distinctive perspective you bring to practitioner concerns. Here you can harvest the content you've been producing during the Investment Phase and assemble it into an opus.

As your authority status grows, people will start seeking you out for advice and guidance. Doors will start to open for you. This is when you can start harvesting and taking full advantage of the hard work you did during the investment period. Your influence becomes catalytic. People want to engage with you directly and begin inviting you to participate at conferences, industry events, and other gatherings. Executives may invite you to train the managers in their organization. Some authorities take advantage of their status by starting a consulting business or offering their services as a coach or mentor to practitioners. At this point, you can move from building your authority to consolidating your reputation and building out your authority enterprise.

Even though you have established yourself as an authority, you still need to continue producing valuable content, keep engaging, and stay on top of the latest trends and developments in your field. What most academic authorities I have interviewed have found is that the self-sustaining virtuous cycle emerges in the late stages of the Liftoff Phase. As opportunities to participate with practitioners multiply, you are constantly re-engaging with managers. As you do so, you have new opportunities to discover emergent issues and trends that keep you on the cutting edge of the field, serving as data for your next content cycle.

The Maintenance Phase

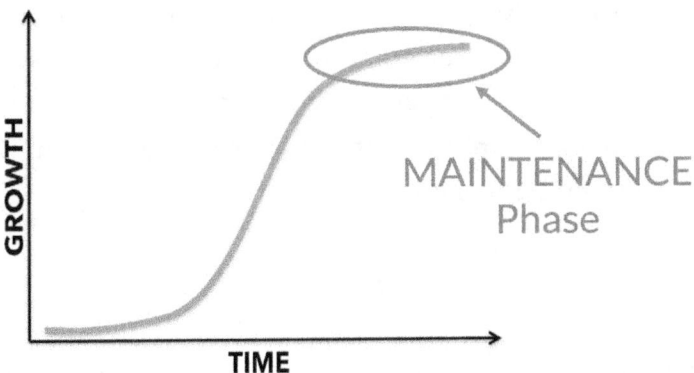

During the Maintenance Phase, you have established momentum and don't have to work as hard to maintain your authority status. You've achieved the self-reinforcing stage of authority. People know you; they expect to hear from you; they're looking for your latest thoughts or solutions, be it your next book, article, or commentary on what is happening in the industry. This phase is akin to a flywheel. You've worked hard to get the flywheel spinning. But once it's in motion, you need only give it a rhythmic tap occasionally to maintain its momentum.

What does maintaining momentum look like? To illustrate, I'll share some examples from my own experience. I share these stories not to impress you but to impress upon you what is possible when you reach the Maintenance Phase. As I have mentioned before, I am a very unlikely authority, but I did work hard to learn and do the right things on a consistent basis to reach liftoff and create self-sustaining momentum.

In one example, I had collaborated with a colleague from Yale on an article about non-market strategy and how companies were responding to social movements during the COVID-19 era. We wanted to publish quickly because the message was timely, so we explored venues other than *HBR* or *MIT Sloan*, which tend to have long publication processes. After reviewing reader demographics on the Rotman School of Management's journal, we found that they were reaching tens of thousands of executives that aligned with our desired profile. Despite never having published with this journal and having no prior contacts with the publishers, we decided to pursue it.

Not knowing the editor personally, I created an inquiry email and addressed it to the "editor@rotman.utoronto," a cold-call approach that, in many instances, goes ignored or gets placed at the bottom of the editorial queue. I also attached a complete draft of the article. The email illustrates how I used momentum in the outreach.

The email said:

"My name is Gregory Unruh, and I am an admirer of your journal. I'm also a contributor to MIT Sloan Management Review. *I say that so you have some sense of the kind of writing and articles I tend to publish. I have written a piece I think might fit in with your editorial thrust and have attached a copy for your review. I enjoy working with smart editors and appreciate the valuable feedback that always leads to a stronger piece that*

speaks to the journal's audience. So, expect me to be collaborative, should you choose to move ahead.

Thanks in advance for your consideration.
Best, Gregory

You can see what I did there. First, I complemented and recognized the value of the journal and the editor's work. Then I leaned immediately into my established authority, letting the editor know where I have published before. I could have also sent links to the articles, but it did not seem necessary at this point. I then indicated I had experience working with editors and that I would be collaborative in the publication process. The day after sending the inquiry, I received the following message:

Hi Gregory, thanks so much for submitting this. It's a perfect fit for our Winter Journal World 2.0. The issue comes out around December 15th and mails the first week of January. I would love to add this to the lineup.

Upon receiving the message, my co-author and I were very happy and also sort of shocked that we were greenlighted literally overnight. But such is the power of momentum and the confidence it engenders. The critical mass of presence and content you produce speaks for you, facilitating access and opening doors that are closed to other people.

Another example of momentum in the Maintenance Phase occurred recently when I was contacted about delivering an executive-education session at a top European business school for a major global financial institution. The executive-education director was having a hard time finding someone with the requisite expertise and the authoritative presence needed for a demanding executive audience. As often happens in the Maintenance Phase, someone who had seen me teach in another executive program recommended me, and the program director reached out to me cold by email. Many of the authorities I spoke with told similar stories, that, as the word gets out about your work and impact, you will discover people coming to find you.

ACADEMIC AUTHORITY

Normally after this initial contact, a lengthy vetting process would commence, often requiring more than one meeting, in which a prospect is evaluated by the program directors and the client. So, I inquired about meeting logistics with the executive-education director, as well as the chief learning officer of the bank. This is where the power of momentum showed itself. The executive-education director responded with the following email message:

Dear Gregory,

Thank you for the heads-up, and no worries about the meeting with the client.
They are happy to have you after they saw your credentials with profile and videos.
I'm looking forward to attending your session, as I'm already talking about you with other potential clients!

As you can see, the critical mass of content and materials I had produced during the Investment and Liftoff Phases had established my authority status with a demanding client, without the client ever having to meet me. It also facilitated my introduction to the program leadership at a top executive-education program. Within the hour of the first email, I received a second message from the program coordinator:
Executive-education coordinator to me:

Dear Gregory,

The director mentioned that the client has full trust in you and no meeting is required. I am preparing the lecturer contract for you tomorrow, so it should be with you then. And the calendar invite for Thursday afternoon should be with you any minute.
Please let me know if you have any other questions.

That is the power of momentum. Once you are established, it becomes less labor-intensive to maintain your status. And your relative celebrity among your audience leads to financially and professionally rewarding opportunities that have the added benefit of bringing you back into contact with the very executives you want and need to engage with.

Getting to Liftoff

My goal with this book is to walk you through the steps necessary to reach the Liftoff Phase. I want you to get to a point where your authority and presence begin to reinforce each other, providing a solid foundation for you to expand your academic career into broader professional horizons and opportunities. What you do after liftoff is also very important and is a worthy subject for another book.

Traveling the Authority Development Trajectory requires dedication and effort. As the old saying goes, when opportunity knocks and you open the door, what you find on the other side is hard work. This journey is no different—it demands perseverance and commitment.

I should note that these opportunities are not guaranteed for everyone. Success in reaching liftoff and building a self-reinforcing authority status may come more readily to some than others. It took me years and many missteps. But as I have said, I believe you are in a better position than I was. This book can help equip you with the knowledge and strategies to navigate this path more effectively and efficiently than I did.

While this path offers the potential for new opportunities, outcomes are possibilities rather than promises. Your journey will be uniquely shaped by your individual efforts and circumstances. My hope is that they become tales you will look forward to telling me about.

• • •

PART II

The Authority Framework

CHAPTER 5

The Authority Map

*"If you don't know where you are going,
any road will get you there."*
— Lewis Carroll

*"The map is not the territory,
but it is essential for navigating it."*
—Alfred Korzybski

So far, we have covered the foundational issues of authority, including motivations and mindset. We've also covered the trajectory you can expect as you pursue your authority journey. In Part II of the book, we focus on the actual methods academic authorities use as they engage in practitioner-focused research and publishing. This brief introductory chapter provides an overview of the steps we will cover in Part II.

Based on my interviews with our guru peers and my own experiences, I have distilled the authority process down to four basic steps, illustrated in the graphic on page 66. The steps progress from left to right and build toward you creating value as an authority. Some of you will be satisfied here, extending your scholarship into the managerial realm. However, some of you will be interested in learning how authorities can capture value for themselves, and this is covered in Part III of the book.

The Steps to Authority

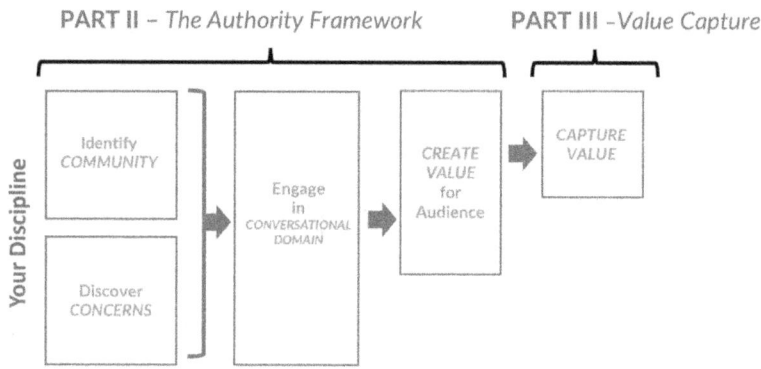

As the figure illustrates, your progress begins with your disciplinary training and expertise, which makes sense, given the years you've spent mastering this area. But all that training is only the beginning of your journey to becoming an academic authority. You will need to go beyond your academic training to address most novel and emerging problems facing your practitioner audience. You may choose to emphasize your disciplinary lens, but it's essential to choose a topic that you are passionate about. Enthusiasm drives your efforts and tends to spark a charismatic energy that can be very persuasive.

The second step, which I cover in Chapter 6, requires identifying a specific community that you want to serve. An authority must have an audience. You will need to find a community of practitioners within your topic that you'll enjoy spending time with. Ideally, it's an organized industry or sector that has established activities, such as conferences, a trade journal, professional training programs, certifications, and so on. Given my interest in environmentalism, I chose to focus on sustainable business organizations.

Once you've identified your community, you will then immerse yourself in their world to discover their current concerns, problems, ambitions, and goals. These then become the issues and aspirations you address. As you are immersed, you can begin engaging in value-added conversations with your audience (see Chapter 7). This requires learning your community's conversational domain or professional jargon so that you can speak to them in their own language. I'll also reveal efficient ways to create influential content so that you can build your presence in the minds of your audience with a minimum of effort.

As you engage with your community, you will discover their most pressing problems. Authorities begin creating real value by providing guidance that allows practitioners to confront and resolve these challenges. You will need to communicate these solutions in an influential manner that reflects your unique perspective and character, which you have been developing during the investment phase. (See Chapters 8 and 9.)

These fundamental steps covered in Part II build upon one another and elevate you to a status of authority among your community and target audience. They are essential to building your authority profile, but they also contribute to a certain type of lifestyle that comes with establishing yourself as an authority, a lifestyle of growth and contribution that brings status and ongoing variety as you connect and contribute to your profession and the world.

• • •

CHAPTER 6

Connecting with Communities and Their Concerns

"If misery loves company, then triumph demands an audience."
— Brian Moore, novelist

Academics and authorities have differing reference points to guide their research. Academics start with concerns dictated by their discipline—questions that respond to the field's current theoretical paradigms. While this approach ensures that academics contribute to scholarly debates, it does not ensure that findings will have practical applications for practitioner audiences. Authorities, by contrast, begin by focusing on a specific community they intend to serve. They immerse themselves in understanding the community's issues, needs, and challenges. Their research contributions are driven by the problems currently facing their audience. The work is often interdisciplinary and integrative, relying upon feedback from the community to ensure relevance to evolving issues.

Leaning on the community to drive your research questions makes sense because the notions of "communities" and "concerns" are essentially two sides of the same coin. If there's a concern, it means there is someone, or some community, behind that concern. Authorities benefit a community by clarifying concerns and complex problems with systematic solution formulas that practitioners can use to tackle their problems in a stepwise manner. This systemization also enables authorities to communicate and teach solutions efficiently.

I've found that many of the frameworks and examples I've published in *Harvard Business Review* and *MIT Sloan Management Review* articles have come directly from engaging with communities. Attending conferences and forums allowed me to hear firsthand the challenges executives were facing and meet the managers who were not only struggling with these issues but were also willing to collaborate and engage with me. These interactions often led to opportunities for case writing and teaching, where I could investigate real-world problems and explore practical solutions. This resulted in solutions that could be applied broadly, helping companies navigate challenges with more confidence and insight. Ettenson at Thunderbird notes that applicability goes even farther: "This is true even between different sectors. The best solutions are often 'industry agnostic.'" Even if you're not a specific industry expert, you can see similarities in challenges across industry sectors. By directly interacting with practitioners, you can ensure that the work is relevant across the business world.

What is interesting is that, by engaging this way, you find yourself becoming a leader in the community's eyes. In fact, many successful authorities become invested in the community they are serving. They become a known, identifiable character, thanks to a unique perspective that differentiates them from other experts and builds name recognition.

The first phase of development is establishing your authority foundation. An authority invests in *building* and *synthesizing* knowledge about a community by immersing in the language, trends, culture, and perspectives of an industry. This mastery not only helps the authority provide contextually relevant insights but also helps them forge meaningful connections with industry professionals This is part of the investment phase, discussed in Chapter 4, which covers the development trajectory. It can take six to eighteen months to build your understanding of a community and develop your unique perspective and communication style.

Learning the Conversational Domain

As you immerse yourself in a community, you will find that there is a unique conversational domain that, if mastered, allows you to engage and communicate in persuasive ways with your audiences. A conversational domain is a set of carefully chosen terms, connected in a systematic way, that allow a specific group of people to have contextualized and efficient conversations. The terminology intrinsic to a sector and the unique set of technical terms, acronyms, and jargon are not just words but also symbols of deeper processes, concepts, and practices specific to the field. All professions have their own conversational domain.

As academics, we've been indoctrinated within our own scholarly and disciplinary conversational domains and can share terms like "information asymmetries" or "institutional isomorphisms" with other academics without a second thought. However, the practitioners we're going to speak with haven't learned our academic conversational domain. And they're not *going* to learn it. To engage with practitioners, you have to learn their conversational domain, a task that requires curiosity and commitment. "I don't see any substitute for understanding the real problem other than spending twenty days in conversations with senior executives," Dartmouth's Vijay Govindarajan told me. "That requires an investment in time. And more than just time, it requires a mindset that values interacting with executives." For Govindarajan, becoming an academic authority makes the investment worthwhile.

Developing linguistic proficiency allows the academic to communicate their insights and contributions in ways that are more accessible and relevant to industry professionals. But beyond the lexical aspects, the conversational domain includes being attuned to the current challenges in the industry.

An Industry's Point of View

I have found that academics who understand a community's unique cultural aspects and can articulate them in an inspiring manner build rapport, respect, and trust. Again, we are using "community" broadly here, meaning the community of practitioners you intend to serve and not any specific industry per se. A place to start in mastering the community's conversational domain is to recognize that each community has a point of view, or POV. We can use POV as a simple framework to distill some key community aspects into *purpose, objectives*, and *values*. These encapsulate the "why," "what," and "how" of the community.

The *purpose* of a community speaks to the profession's "why," providing a clear and compelling reason for the community's existence. This is the superordinate goal of the profession, its higher societal purpose. Disciplines have these, of course. The purpose of law, for example, is justice. For medicine, it's human health. But industries and professions have them as well. The purpose of the Institute of Electrical and Electronics Engineers (IEEE), whose members are professionals in the electronics and computing fields, for example, is to foster technological innovation for the benefit of humanity. Authorities who can clearly articulate and remind an audience of its higher purpose and its service to society take on the mantle of leadership.

All professions and associations also have *objectives* that address the "what" of the community's doing. Objectives translate a community's higher purpose into actionable strategies that facilitate planning and enable the measurement of progress. They guide resource allocation, ensuring that efforts and investments are channeled effectively toward activities that are congruent with the community's purpose. In the case of the American Marketing Association (AMA), objectives translate into actionable programs and services for members, including professional-development courses and national conferences to train and inform members. The AMA also conducts industry research and advocates for marketing professionals' interests. Authorities can also assess and speak to these objectives, often with the intention of helping practitioners achieve their goals faster or inspiring them to go beyond traditional goals to expand the possibilities of the community.

Finally, the *values* articulate the "how"—the responsibilities the community maintains as it pursues its purpose and objectives. Values are the bedrock of a community's culture and ethical framework. They inform decision-making, ensuring that actions and initiatives align with these core principles. This cultural foundation is crucial for building a strong, positive internal environment, fostering member loyalty, and enhancing collaboration. The ethical framework provided by these values is also vital in maintaining integrity, public trust, and in resolving conflicts, as it offers a consistent and principled approach to handling challenges and disputes. For the IEEE, the community values include integrity, excellence, and respect for individuals' rights and interests, fostering an environment where innovation thrives on ethical and professional foundations.

In my early days of learning to be an authority in sustainability, the field of business sustainability was still in its infancy. I saw a need to help articulate the emerging themes that would define the sustainability conversation. Whether it was environmental stewardship, corporate social responsibility, or sustainable business models, I consciously worked to weave these themes into my writing and speaking. My intention was to help shape the dialogue around sustainability, to move it from being a niche topic to part of a larger business strategy. By highlighting societal contributions and the critical role of technology in advancing sustainable solutions, I was able to connect with both executives and sustainability professionals who were beginning to understand how these issues would impact their work. These efforts not only helped position me as a thought leader but also supported the broader business community in engaging more deeply with sustainability.

Being able to articulate the community's POV in your own way creates a keystone for developing your unique perspective. Your ability to speak to the higher purpose and values can be inspirational and, in many cases, can set you apart as a leading voice in the community. It is a useful starting point as you begin to master the conversational domain of your chosen community. However, it is only a starting point. Authorities delve deeper into their communities through direct engagement with practitioners.

Engaging Practitioners

Once you've identified a community and have become familiar with its conversational domain, you need to find the right managers to work with. The authorities I interviewed made the point that engaging with executives is partially a question of mindset, a desire to lean into the conversational domain. "You have to want to communicate with executives," explained Andrew Campbell of Hult International Business School. "You have to convert your ideas into something that's useful to executives. So, you immerse yourself in the phenomenon in a conversational way. The research you do is talking to executives." This will help you understand their needs and wants, which will enable you to discover solutions that may be useful for them.

One of the challenges academics face is that managers are time-pressed and often hard to access. Fortunately, your immersion in their conversational domain will help you understand the reasons for these time pressures, something that can be brought in service of your outreach. Many executives understand and value what an academic perspective can bring to their problems. "Academics will say that these people are too time pressed, which they are, but get over it. They value insights that will help them do their job better," said George Day, Professor Emeritus at the Wharton School of the University of Pennsylvania.

This interaction isn't just about extracting information; it's a two-way street where you, the academic, contribute your disciplinary expertise while gaining practical insights. When you converse with a manager, you're not just learning about industry practices but also testing and refining your ideas against real-world scenarios. This process enriches your practitioner work, making it more relevant and applied, enhancing your credibility and authority in the field. By approaching executives with the understanding that the engagement will benefit both of you, you will find many executives amenable to engaging.

One business-school authority I interviewed shared a unique approach to refining his ideas by engaging directly with his executive-education participants. He would have them fill out detailed surveys at the start of each program, asking them to identify their biggest leadership challenges in the program's topic areas. By systematically collecting this data, he could better understand the real-world issues these executives faced and test his emerging hypotheses against their experiences. This process not only allowed him to validate his solutions but also helped him refine his frameworks to be more actionable and relevant to the practitioners in his audience. The ability to bridge the gap between theory and practice was enhanced by this feedback loop, ensuring that his teaching remained grounded in the realities of contemporary business challenges, while advancing his solutions.

Like this authority, a good way to begin is by tapping into the network of managers and professionals associated with your institution. If you're in a business school, you already have relationships with businesses. There's a large alumni base that tends to be very interested in reconnecting and speaking with their former professors. Some of these students can become valuable contacts for understanding the day-to-day realities facing managers. Beyond alumni, there are donors, speakers, advisory-board members, recruiters, and others, forming a vast network of relationships you can tap into.

However, you should not limit yourself to these familiar contacts. "Business schools do have relationships with businesses, but I never had any problem just reaching out to people and saying, 'I'm working on this research project; would you be willing to talk to me for a few minutes about it?'" said Babson College's Tom Davenport. "And, in general, they are almost always willing to do it." Many managers feel honored that a professor is interested in their work and, when approached the right way, are open to sharing their perspectives.

Thus, one of the engagement keys is identifying the right type of manager and approaching them with the right mindset. Not all executives will be helpful in advancing your work. "There's actually two kinds of practitioners that we have to remember," said USC's Ann Majchrzak. "There is the crisis-management type, who do small incremental changes." These are the managers who are mostly interested in keeping the trains running on time and making current processes run smoothly. Majchrzak said she is looking for another managerial type: "We're after a different kind. I usually want to speak to what I call *reflective practitioners*. They're thinking about the future that managers are facing." Reflective managers are not satisfied with making sure current systems keep running and are instead constantly thinking at a higher level about what they are doing and looking for opportunities for a breakthrough in performance.

All of the academic authorities I interviewed for this book made the same point, with some calling the target executives "thoughtful managers." The point was clear. Some managers are thinking in a higher, systemic way about their organizations and their work, looking for superior, practical, and often straightforward avenues to achieve their goals. They are also attending to how larger industry and economic trends are likely to play out and impact performance. These managers are a rich resource for academic thought leaders and should be systematically cultivated.

After making contact, you will want to arrange an interview. I have found asking for a small amount of their time, say fifteen to twenty minutes, is a good move. It seems like a very modest commitment on behalf of the manager, but is usually enough time to gather substantial information, especially if you're clear about the problem you're addressing. You will also find that, as the manager warms to the topic, they will give you additional time, but always be respectful and do not abuse this generosity. Whether during in-person interviews or via Zoom or phone, ask if you can record the conversation for transcription, which becomes invaluable for referencing later. Remember that you're not just engaging with this practitioner on a one-time basis. You're beginning to build a network of managers to return to over time. This "Rolodex" of managers is a valuable part of the investment phase. This goes both ways, of course, and you will find yourself becoming part of their "Rolodex" as well.

Identifying and engaging the right type of managers and cultivating mutually beneficial relationships will set a solid foundation for your authority trajectory. Your goal is to serve your community by understanding their objectives and finding ways to assist them in achieving these goals more effectively. The network you build will not only enrich your research and understanding but will also enhance your influence and credibility within the community.

Capturing an Audience

As you progress through the investment phase and immerse yourself in the community and their issues, you will begin to craft your own synthesis of the state of the field and your own unique perspective about the opportunities and challenges facing the community. Of course, it is unlikely that you will ever be as steeped in the industry as your audience, but that is where your value often lies. You bring an objective, authoritative, and external perspective that those immersed in the situation cannot.

As you do this, you can begin cultivating your own audience. Your audience will initially be a subset of the larger community that connects with you and resonates with your unique perspective and message. This audience serves as the cornerstone for establishing influence and disseminating ideas. As should be clear, you are cultivating a symbiotic relationship with your audience. Initially, you are learning from your contacts and synthesizing community insights and solutions. You are also delivering these insights and solutions back to the audience in compelling ways that improve performance. Keeping this bi-directional flow of value in mind is important. In this section, we will cover three primary avenues for audience cultivation: a bestowed audience, a built audience, and a borrowed audience. Each of these approaches offers unique advantages and challenges. They are not mutually exclusive, so understanding how and when to effectively utilize each approach is important.

Bestowed Audiences

The first strategy is to take advantage of the audience that you already have. As a university professor, you have a ready audience in the constituents of your school and its programs, including alumni, donors, and the like. But, through your faculty position, your institution bestows upon you a captive audience of students. You are already serving this audience by transferring disciplinary knowledge to them, but you can think strategically about how to gain full advantage from this opportunity. As the previous example illustrated, many academic authorities find their students are valuable in providing fresh perspectives and insights and also for validating and testing ideas.

Of course, not all students are the same. Most of us start with undergraduate students, who are often eager and open to new ideas but usually lack practical experience. Because of this, they usually do not bring the informed understanding needed for insightful conversations that can illuminate the challenges of working professionals. That said, undergraduate audiences are good for refining the presentation of your ideas and perfecting the way you teach your approaches. In refining your approach, no opportunity in front of an audience should be wasted. And you should always keep in mind that today's undergraduate student is tomorrow's senior executive. Following the progress and successes of your students is mutually rewarding and allows you to cultivate potentially important future contacts for expanding your practitioner network.

Undergraduates are fine, but your plan should be to systematically move up the seniority hierarchy. Business-school programs are arranged in a hierarchical manner from undergraduate to MBA to Executive MBA and executive-education programs. Your goal should be to strategically ascend this pyramid.

The next progression after undergrads is teaching MBA students, who usually have a few years of work experience, offering more informed feedback and engagement. One of the best practices is to use the case-teaching method with your MBAs. Case teaching fosters a unique set of skills that is beneficial to authorities. It hones facilitation skills, transitioning from the traditional lecture-based teaching model to a role where you guide and stimulate discussions. This shift demands a keen ability to manage conversational dynamics. Moreover, the case method enhances your listening and observational skills. You must attentively listen to student contributions, observe classroom interactions, and understand nuanced perspectives. This heightened attention is important for extracting key learning moments and connecting diverse viewpoints. You will find your critical-thinking and problem-solving skills are also sharpened, as you encourage students to navigate complex case scenarios and propose solutions to real-world business challenges. And, of course, the case method builds storytelling and narrative skills, helping you present ideas in an engaging manner. These skills are all foundational parts of an authority's skill set.

The culmination of this progression is teaching executive MBAs and engaging in executive-education programs. You can significantly bolster your authority by effectively utilizing executive-education audiences. Teaching in executive-education programs can be transformative. Ex-ed participants typically have substantial industry experience, making them similar to the ultimate audience you are trying to reach—seasoned professionals in decision-making roles. These participants not only provide informed feedback but also enable you, the academic, to understand practical industry challenges and perspectives. The interaction is a two-way street of learning and influence. The reciprocal engagement allows you to fine-tune solutions to be more industry-relevant and applicable, enhancing your credibility and authority within the field.

Some academics treat teaching as secondary to research, but this would be a mistake for academic authorities. Each interaction and teaching experience offers a chance to hone your skills, build your network, and deepen your understanding of the challenges and dynamics within your field from the practitioner audience you seek to cultivate.

Built Audiences

A second strategy is building your own audience. Social-media platforms have made it possible for anyone to build their own audience through content creation and distribution via online platforms like YouTube, Twitter (X), LinkedIn, and Instagram. Building an audience through social media, popular among "influencers," represents a distinct approach. This method typically involves consistently building a YouTube channel, maintaining an active feed on X (formerly Twitter), and engaging on Facebook and LinkedIn. While effective, this approach can be akin to a full-time job due to the constant need for content creation, promotion, and audience engagement.

I found that this is not the most efficient and effective way for academic authorities to capture an audience. That does not mean social-media platforms do not have a role to play. But beware using them as the foundation of your authority platform. That said, some academics find success using this approach. A colleague of mine, Tyler Cohen, an economist and co-director of the Mercatus Center at George Mason University, exemplifies this approach. He uses his expertise in economics to offer a unique perspective on a wide range of issues, including government policy, globalization, food, and the arts.

He cultivated his audience with a blog titled "Marginal Revolution," which he co-authors with a colleague. The blog is highly regarded for its commentary on economic theory and current events. He expanded his influence further as director of the Mercatus Institute, creating an interview series called "Conversations with Tyler," in which he engages in podcast-style interviews with influential figures across different fields, something that not only creates excellent content for his audience but also serves as a continuous source of new information. It allows him to further build his authority and deepen his expertise by interacting with and learning from leading experts. The consistent production of quality content caught the attention of *The New York Times* and an invitation for Cohen to contribute a column called "Economic Scene" on an ongoing basis.

Cohen's trajectory illustrates the potential of building an online platform to engage and cultivate an audience. However, it's important to reiterate that such an endeavor requires dedication to consistently produce content that resonates with and adds value to the intended audience.

Borrowed Audiences

As discussed, many communities assembled around interests, such as supply chains, finance, and marketing, already exist. Instead of starting from scratch to build your own audience, why not borrow someone else's? In other words, attract an audience from an existing community.

The place to start is by looking for industry associations in your field of expertise with large professional memberships. Associations provide several advantages for an authority during the investment phase. They know the community well, including their goals, problems, and pressing issues. They are often the keepers of the community's POV. Also, they usually produce white papers, blogs, and other information on their website that you can use to immerse yourself quickly in the community. Additionally, because they tend to want to attract advertisers, they have collected demographic information on these communities that they make readily available. The association also serves as an established distribution network to the community. They usually have organized events, including conferences, local networking events, webinars, and training programs. Attending these events exposes you to the most pressing issues faced by the community, presented by the practitioners themselves. They are also usually receptive to the engagement of academics.

When I was building my authority in sustainable business, I reached out to associations like Sustainable Brands, GreenBiz, the World Business Council for Sustainable Development (WBCSD), and the United Nations Global Compact, to inquire how academics could get involved. More often than not, they would offer free or deeply discounted access to events, sometimes inviting me to serve as a panelist or to write articles that they would distribute to their members. Attending their events gave me direct access and insights for refining my own work, as well as a platform for me to connect with and contribute to the community. This provided a ready-made network of professionals, from which I could start building my own audience.

Your goal in the investment and synthesis phase is to efficiently establish yourself as an expert among a network of practitioners and to cultivate an audience that resonates with your perspective. Associations accelerate this process. Consider it a form of authority leverage, which I discuss next.

Authority Leverage

The last section of this chapter is dedicated to helping you establish yourself in your community as efficiently as possible. To do so, we will use the idea of leverage. Leverage is a fundamental strategy in finance and investment. At its core, leverage involves utilizing borrowed capital to increase the potential return of your own investment. This approach amplifies the buying power of an investor, allowing them to control larger assets than would be possible with their own funds alone. You do this when you buy a house by using a mortgage to purchase a property with a minimal down payment. In the vernacular of investing, this is a process of using Other People's Money, or OPM.

In the journey of an academic authority, there are two types of leverage to be had. The first is a different type of OPM: Other People's Minds (OPM). The second is OPA, or Other People's Audiences.

Tapping into Other People's Minds is what you are doing when you are engaging with practitioners in your interviews and conversations. This form of leverage is about accessing the intelligence, experiences, and insights of industry practitioners. Academics can gain significant leverage by understanding real-world challenges, trends, and the practices of practitioners. You also do this by extracting the core insights from industry associations and their membership.

As discussed, some executives—exactly the type you want to cultivate as part of your network—are often adept at synthesizing issues and even naming emerging concerns. I recall one instance when an executive casually mentioned the term "private label sustainability" to describe a trend he observed in which companies were creating their own certification systems to measure the sustainability performance of their products. I recognized the clarity of this term, I asked if I could use it, and he readily agreed. I began incorporating "private label sustainability" into my presentations, and it immediately resonated with audiences. The phrase captured an evolving issue in a way that was clear and actionable for practitioners, helping to frame an emerging trend that more companies were beginning to explore.

You'll also gain leverage by accessing Other People's Audiences, particularly by integrating yourself into industry associations and networks. This approach is much more efficient than trying to build an audience from scratch. There are a number of ways you can benefit from OPA. Attending events hosted by industry associations can be an exceptionally efficient and powerful method for quickly gaining insights into the concerns and dynamics of a professional community. These events, ranging from international conferences to local networking events to webinars to training programs, offer a wealth of opportunities to learn about the issues these organizations face. By attending talks and presentations, academics can hear directly from practitioners, providing a firsthand understanding of the challenges within the industry. Moreover, such events are prime opportunities for conducting high-quality interviews. In just a few days at a conference, for instance, you can immerse yourself in the community and capture a dozen or more valuable interviews that can be integrated into research.

In one memorable instance of OPM and OPA, I reached out to Ethical Corporation because they were hosting a conference on the emerging issue of business and NGO collaborations. As usual, I inquired about whether they would waive the registration fee, which was several thousand dollars, for me since I was an academic. Instead of a simple yes or no, I was passed to the event organizer, who proposed a different opportunity: They suggested that I attend and write a summary report on the event, which they would distribute to their thousands of members with my name as the expert author.

Sensing a bigger opportunity, I countered with an additional request. I asked if I could bring a small team of MBA students with me to help cover the event, and they agreed. Enabled by this partnership, I attended the conference with my students. We fanned out to take notes during the sessions, meeting each evening to debrief and discuss what we were learning. It was a great learning and networking opportunity for my students. By the end of the event, the organizers gave us a disk with all the presentation slides and recordings of all of the sessions.

We produced a comprehensive report on the state of business-NGO collaborations, which was circulated throughout the Ethical Corporation's member network and got even larger media coverage. This experience raised my profile in the community substantially, positioning me as a practical expert on a rapidly developing issue. I used what I learned and the contacts I made to produce a series of case studies and some practitioner articles on business-NGO collaboration. Not only that, but the experience was transformative for my students as well—half of them received job offers from connections they made during the conference. It was a massive win for all involved.

These OPM and OPA interactions are more than just information-gathering sessions; they're a chance for a deep dive that is not only informative but also central in developing a nuanced understanding of an industry's landscape. In most instances, these associations will be enthusiastic about academics participating and will often offer complimentary access to what would otherwise be a very expensive event. Still, there are costs involved in traveling to an event and covering food and lodging, which may be out of reach for some academics. Fortunately, in today's post-Covid world, many associations now offer virtual events, providing access to telecast sessions, webinars, and recorded presentations from past events. These online resources can be just as informative and insightful. By strategically utilizing these resources, academics can quickly gain the capacity to authoritatively speak on what's happening in the community and begin contributing their unique perspectives to the field.

Once you are established in the community and become a known quantity to association leadership, you will be in a position to access the association community through their communications channels. This then gives you direct access to professionals that you are interested in speaking to. It also provides an opportunity for you to cultivate your own audience, which will be a subset of the larger association membership.

Successful engagement with a community is a powerful way to accelerate your academic-thought-leader trajectory. It not only helps in grasping the community's conversational domain but also in focusing you on significant problems and developing clear, concise solutions. However, it is important to recognize that not everyone in the community will align with your perspective. This is actually a good thing. Don't try to be everything to everyone. Your goal should be to attract an audience that resonates with your approach while naturally distancing yourself from those who do not. Therefore, carefully consider whom you aim to serve, and tailor your communication to attract the right individuals. Your authority character is a useful tool in doing this. Creating a clear persona that symbolizes your authority approach will provide a mental shortcut for association members and will help attract the audience you want and help you to distance yourself from those who are not aligned with your perspectives.

The synthesis of engagement and understanding forms the bedrock of your expertise, enabling you to speak authoritatively about community issues and contribute your unique perspective to the dialogue. Find more on that in the next chapter.

・・・

CHAPTER 7

Engaging in Value-added Conversations

"The only way to avoid criticism is to do nothing, say nothing, and be nothing."
— Elbert Hubbard

"Strive not to be a success, but rather to be of value."
— Albert Einstein

In this chapter, I'll focus on how you can engage in conversations with your community and audience in ways that they find valuable. We will do so in an efficient and synergistic way that helps advance your mastery of the conversational domain and synthesis of the field, while also building your profile and reputation as a go-to thought leader in your community. You will be using mostly internet-based publishing platforms and social media in targeted ways to reach your audience. If you search online, you will find that there are many "experts" out there that have their own "secret" formulas for interacting with people and building a following online. Some of their advice is useful, and some is problematic. What I will share here is what I have learned about what serves us as academic thought leaders. The goal is to find out where your target audience is already congregating and enter into their conversations in ways that add value and demonstrate your knowledge and unique perspective. And, of course, to do this in the most time-efficient manner possible.

For starters, you'll need your own authority website, which will be the main hub and contact point for your audience. Don't worry—setting up a website is easier than you might think, and getting easier with new artificial-intelligence tools.

Next, we will look at curation as an efficient method for you to stay abreast of events and trends in your sector, while also cultivating your audience and building your presence in your community. This is part of the Investment and Synthesis phase of your authority-development trajectory. You are developing the skills of an academic authority while synthesizing the field and adding value for your audience.

Your Digital Authority Platform

So that you are easily accessible and can efficiently share your insights, you will need to establish your digital platform. This will be a combination of a personal-branded website and select social media accounts. What you are building is a content-syndication system. Syndication is the process of republishing your content across multiple platforms to expand your reach and maximize impact. Syndication originally comes from the newspaper and media industries, where content—such as articles, comic strips, and columns—was licensed and distributed to multiple publications to reach a broader audience. Rather than relying solely on your own website or blog, a content-syndication system strategically places your work in high-visibility outlets where your target audience already congregates. The system is illustrated in the graphic on page 87, which may initially look daunting but really has only 3 components: 1) your own authority website, 2) a microblogging platform, and 3) a couple of select social-media accounts that align with your communication styles.

Engaging in Value-added Conversations

The Content Syndication System

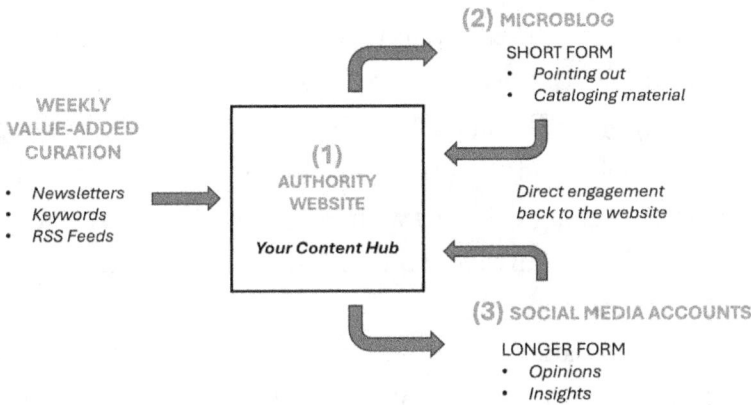

You should start with a personal website as your homebase and headquarters. Having a website is necessary because it offers a level of control and permanence that cannot be achieved with social media platforms. Owning your own site provides a stable and customizable digital space that serves as a centralized repository for your work, insights, and content. Unlike social-media accounts, which are subject to changing algorithms and the policies of external management, a personal website affords complete autonomy over content and presentation. This independence ensures that your work is shared exactly as intended, free from third-party interference.

You should also integrate a "blog" into your personal website. I use the term "blog" here loosely. Broadly speaking, a blog (short for "weblog") is an ongoing vehicle for delivering your content and insights via your website. You may create written posts, or you may prefer spoken podcasts or a video-based vlog (video log) format. The format you choose will depend on your personal preferences and style. It will also depend on your audience and which channels are best for reaching them. You will support your website with a small number of appropriately selected social-media accounts, such as LinkedIn, X (formerly Twitter), Facebook, and Instagram.

When I first started building my authority, I created a blog on my personal website, where I started posting articles and videos on sustainability and related business topics. After each post, I would push the link to my blog out on my social-media accounts, such as LinkedIn and Twitter, to increase visibility and drive traffic back to my site. However, things shifted once my *Harvard Business Review* Press book was published. With the credibility of the book and examples of the blog posts I had written, I reached out to larger platforms like *Huffington Post* and *Forbes*, inquiring about contributing to their publications. My book and my published content were compelling enough that I was offered ongoing columns with both outlets. This step significantly expanded my reach and further solidified my status as a thought leader in the sustainability space.

While you will broadcast your work through social media, always direct people back to your website as your official outlet. It is the foundation of your digital footprint and helps you create visibility in search-engine results through a recognizable professional online presence. A website and blog empower you with control and stability, something that the transient and limited nature of social media cannot fully provide.

In addition to your website headquarters, you should also establish select social-media accounts dedicated solely to your authority communications, keeping them separate from any personal social-media accounts.

The choice of the platforms will depend mostly on your audience. Choose platforms where your audience is already congregating and engaging in conversations about work and industry. The right outlets should become obvious as you do your research about your community, but you can find published statistics about platforms and their users. This can be very helpful in understanding their behavior and targeting your audience. For example, if you wanted to reach a conservative audience, a quick review of the social-media platform Truth Social would show that the audience is overwhelmingly conservative men. That's fine if that is your target, but if you also want to reach women, you will find surveys that say 73% of women say they won't use the site. Spending some time investigating platforms is a worthwhile time investment.

Social-media accounts also tend to have different functionalities. Some are text-based, while others privilege photography, images, or video. While there has been a trend toward convergence in social media, with differing

The Authority Website

Your thought-leader website should be strategically designed to highlight expertise, credibility, and a unique value proposition. Here's a sample outline of what a website could encompass:

- **Professional and engaging design**: The website should have a clean, modern design that reflects your authority character discussed previously. It should be easy to navigate, with a clear structure that guides visitors to the most important information. This is where you can show people your authority persona.

- **Prominent biography**: The homepage should feature a brief but impactful biography that succinctly highlights your authority-positioning stack discussed in the previous chapter.

- **Content:** You can showcase your expertise and engage a broader audience by featuring content on your personal website through blogs, videos, podcasts, and downloadable resources that bridge academic insights with practical applications for professionals.

- **Highlighted speaking engagements**: A showcase of past speaking engagements you cultivate, including keynote speeches, panels, workshops, and seminars. You should include videos, summaries, or testimonials from event organizers or attendees. You don't need many of these; three is a great place to begin, so you should be actively seeking these out as you move along your trajectory.

- **Media and press**: A compilation of media appearances, interviews, and articles written by or featuring you. This section serves to enhance credibility and showcase your ability to engage with a wider audience.

- **Calls-to-action**: Clear calls-to-action (CTAs) inviting inquiries for speaking, coaching, or consulting engagements, including a contact form, email address, and/or phone number.

- **Testimonials and endorsements**: Positive feedback from peers, clients, and collaborators you have cultivated, highlighting your skills as a speaker, consultant, thought leader, and so on. Again, three endorsements is a good and attainable early goal.

- **Contact information**: Easy-to-find contact details for professional inquiries, and a simple, straightforward contact form.

Your website should serve as a compelling digital portfolio that not only displays your qualifications and achievements but also effectively communicates your value proposition to potential clients and event organizers. The focus should be on demonstrating how your expertise can add value, solve problems, and provide insightful perspectives to your communities. Website development is becoming much easier with emerging AI tools, so be sure to investigate the latest developments in this rapidly progressing field.

platforms adding similar functions, think carefully about each platform you choose, because they will serve different communication roles.

Your first account should be a *microblogging* tool. Microblogging is used for posting short messages, images, or video links to share information quickly and interactively with an audience. The original microblog is Twitter, and it is the reason we call microblog posts "tweets." Since Elon Musk's 2022 acquisition, Twitter has been rebranded X. Facebook has a competing microblog called Threads. Tumblr is another notable platform. Additionally, platforms like Instagram and Pinterest, while primarily image-based, also allow microblogging through captions and hashtags that enable quick, visually driven communication.

Authorities use microblogging to enhance their visibility, share knowledge, and engage with a broader audience. Microblogging is also useful for networking and collaboration, as you can follow and interact with peers, industry experts, and organizations to build relationships. You can also engage with followers through discussions, Q&A sessions, or polls. Some authorities will do things like live-tweet during conferences or seminars to provide real-time insights to their followers. Importantly, microblogging can be used to drive traffic to your website for more detailed content.

An example of an authority who uses microblogging is Wharton School professor Adam Grant. Grant leverages Twitter to share concise insights from his research on leadership, psychology, and organizational behavior. By posting thought-provoking content, he engages his large following and sparks discussions on relevant topics. He also live-tweets during conferences and seminars, offering real-time insights to his audience, making exclusive events more accessible as well as highlighting his presence at elite confabs. He also uses Twitter to drive traffic to his more-detailed articles, podcasts, and blog posts, connecting microblogging with long-form content. This strategy has helped him build an audience of more than 500,000 followers, enhancing his visibility and solidifying his reputation as a thought leader in the business world.

While potentially powerful, these platforms can also become black holes that suck up time and attention. That's why a strategy is essential. I recommend using microblogs for what I call "pointing." It's like using your finger to direct attention to a particular article or event. With Twitter, you don't have much space (280 characters), so it's efficient for highlighting relevant content without lengthy elaboration. You simply point your audience toward something they should be aware of, without diving into detailed analysis. For example, you might tweet: "All HR professionals should pay attention to this [linked article] because of Y." You're directing people to the resource, emphasizing its relevance without providing deep commentary.

ACADEMIC AUTHORITY

A real-world example of this from my own account is:

(@gregoryunruh): *"While unsurprising, this demonstrates the importance for financial institutions of ensuring that capital provided to firms in the real economy is invested in accordance with net-zero goals and does not lead to carbon lock-in." [Link to Article: Critical Role of Cost of Capital in Net-Zero Transitions].*

Here, I briefly point to the significance of an article on climate policy and finance, linking it to my work on Carbon Lock-in, without extensive discussion.

Pointing like this serves two purposes. First, you are connecting with your audience on an ongoing basis by sharing what you find noteworthy. Your short commentary allows you to demonstrate your unique perspective and express your authority character. Second, because there is a continuous record of your tweets, you are also building a repository of interesting articles and examples for your own reference. In the above example, I both pointed my audience to an interesting article and also effectively saved it for later reference. I have relied on my Twitter feed to save interesting case examples, quotes, research, and stories for personal reference and for use in presentations and publications. With a list of posts like this, you can return to your feed at any time to access content and examples, something that is invaluable when you are creating more elaborated materials.

For longer format content, you will need an additional social-media platform. For most of you, this will be LinkedIn, the leading professional social-networking site. Another option is Medium, a platform popular with professionals and many journalists. LinkedIn is superior for its professional-networking capabilities, which provide opportunities to both disseminate content and also build meaningful connections within an industry. LinkedIn allows for the direct publication of articles to share in-depth insights and expert analyses on topics. The site also segments the larger professional audience into LinkedIn Groups, so that you can ensure your work reaches a targeted audience of professionals seeking the latest research and expert opinions to inform their decision-making processes.

Long-Format Online Content Platforms

PLATFORM	PROS	CONS	BEST FOR
LinkedIn	- Strong **professional networking** and audience targeting. - Content reaches **executives, managers, and industry leaders**. - High **SEO ranking** and discoverability. - Can share in **LinkedIn Groups** for niche exposure.	- Primarily **business-focused**; less engagement from academic audiences. - Content is **not easily shareable outside LinkedIn**.	**Professors engaging with professionals, executives, and industry leaders.**
Medium	- **Wider reach** beyond professional circles. - **Algorithm-driven discovery** for potential virality. - **Easy to use** and visually clean format.	- **Less networking potential** than LinkedIn. - **Limited targeting**; no segmented professional groups.	**Public thought leadership and interdisciplinary engagement.**
Substack	- **Direct audience control** via email subscriptions. - Ability to **monetize content** through paid subscriptions. - **Long-term audience building** rather than relying on algorithms.	- Requires **consistent content creation** to maintain subscribers. - Less **organic discovery** compared to Medium or LinkedIn.	**Academics who want direct engagement and control over their audience.**

For one of our annual sustainable business reports in collaboration with *MIT Sloan Management Review* and Boston Consulting Group, I created a LinkedIn series that highlighted specific findings from the research. One of the initial articles, "What Is a Sustainability Strategy?" emphasized a key finding from our eight-year-long project. Another article in the series, "3 Types of Materiality for Sustainability Executives," explored the varying definitions of "materiality" being used by sustainability executives. Throughout the series, I focused on breaking down these larger insights from the main report to actionable and informative content appropriate for the platform and audience.

Not everyone likes producing written content. For those of you focusing on podcasts or video content instead of written blogging, you will be using auditory and visual media to engage and grow your audience. When considering social-media outlets for podcasting, platforms like Spotify, Apple Podcasts, and Google Podcasts have vast user bases and the ability to categorize content for easy discovery. For video content, YouTube stands out as a prime channel for its extensive reach and SEO benefits. Short-form media like TikTok and Instagram Reels tend to appeal to a younger demographic through punchy, short videos.

While you will continue to house your content on your website, you will also want to strategically select additional distribution channels that align with your content style and audience preferences.

These three elements—the authority website, microblog, and social media—work together as the foundation of your content-syndication system, with each element complementing the others to enhance your reach and impact. The authority website acts as the central hub, a repository of in-depth, substantial content such as detailed articles, research findings, and educational resources. Microblogging platforms like Twitter come into play for more immediate, concise communication and future references. They are also useful for piquing interest and directing followers to your website hub for longer-format content. Meanwhile, your broader social-media presence on platforms like LinkedIn and YouTube expand the ecosystem leverage to allow more extensive networking, community building, and targeted interaction with your audience. This system ensures that content is disseminated in a variety of formats, reaching audiences where they are most active and engaging them in different ways. The synergy reinforces your status across multiple digital platforms. And you will do so with a minimum of effort, as discussed in the following section.

Value-Added Curation

The approach discussed here teaches you how to leverage content across multiple platforms to create a ubiquitous online presence. As I mentioned, there are many different approaches to this kind of publication. What I present here is the method I found most helpful in building up your authority profile during the investment phases. The method recommended is *content curation*, a process of gathering information on particular topics and sharing it with an audience to add value through selection and elaboration. For establishing your authority status, information curation is a tool for building expertise while mastering your audience's conversational domain. Curation not only enhances your authority positioning, but it also fosters networking opportunities. As you share curated content across platforms, you can attract and engage with an audience.

The curation process can be broken down into three simple steps: *scanning* various information sources, *selecting* appropriate content, and *sharing* it with your community in a value-added format. You can also use *scheduling* to batch your various posts and share them over a longer time period.

The first step involves regularly *scanning* an array of select information sources to gather current and relevant content. You will have discovered many sources during your initial research into your community and topic, and will continue to add sources as you deepen your mastery of the field and conversational domain. Sources can include academic journals, industry news sites, social-media feeds, online databases, and more. This continuous scanning should not be random but targeted toward topics that align with your area of expertise and interests, and meet the needs of your audience. The idea is to cast a net to ensure a broad view of the latest trends, research breakthroughs, debates, and discussions occurring within the field.

In my world of sustainable business, I regularly scan a diverse set of sources to stay informed and relevant. Some of these academic journals, such as *The Journal of Cleaner Production, Organization & Environment* and *Business Strategy and the Environment*, offer the latest peer-reviewed research and thought leadership. I also monitor industry-news platforms like *GreenBiz* and

ACADEMIC AUTHORITY

Sustainable Brands for updates on trends, emerging technologies, and business innovations in sustainability. Additionally, I keep an eye on social-media feeds from key influencers and organizations, such as the World Economic Forum's sustainability team and experts in carbon management, using LinkedIn and Twitter to track relevant discussions. This targeted scanning helps me keep up to date on the most critical issues for my audience.

Marketing professor Richard Ettenson told me he subscribes to many different industry sources, so many, in fact, that his email is jammed with new information every day. This can be overwhelming, so a good approach is to create a separate email from a free account and use it to subscribe to different information newsletters and email services. You can then set up your email with folders that automatically categorize and file the incoming messages for you. When it comes time to check in and review, all of your sources are neatly sorted for you.

Managing digital curation can be further simplified by selecting a suitable aggregator software. News aggregators are digital tools that compile news, articles, and content from various online sources into one accessible platform, making it easier to track topics, trends, and developments across multiple publications. By using these tools, you can efficiently sift through a vast array of information, identify key articles and studies, and stay up to date without the need to individually visit numerous websites or journals. There are many RSS feeds and news aggregators available (See box), and you can choose the one that feels most intuitive to you. Again, you should pay attention to developments in AI that can potentially automate much of this in the near future.

After selecting your aggregator and setting up your account, the next step is to add the high-quality sources relevant to your field that you have identified. Organizing these sources into well-defined categories like "Market Trends," "Academic Research," or "Industry Innovations" streamlines your information intake and makes the process more efficient.

An important information source will be the industry associations related to your field of expertise. If you are specializing in finance, for instance, you might prioritize updates from associations like the American Finance Association or

News Aggregators

Many aggregators use RSS feeds, short for Really Simple Syndication, a type of web feed that allows users to access updates to online content in a standardized, computer-readable format. By subscribing to the RSS feeds of relevant industry blogs, news sites, and industry publications, you can receive automatic updates whenever new content is published. You can use RSS feed aggregators or readers to consolidate multiple feeds into a single, organized interface, making it easier to quickly scan through the latest updates.

Three popular news aggregators for academic thought leaders that are both easy to use and efficient are:

1. **Feedly**: Feedly is a popular choice among academics due to its clean interface and the ability to organize content into customizable feeds. Users can subscribe to various RSS feeds, journals, blogs, and news sources, categorizing them into different topics for easy navigation. It's particularly useful for keeping track of new articles in specific research areas.
2. **Google News**: Google News uses AI algorithms to bring together news from different sources, providing a comprehensive view of the latest headlines and developments. Academics can tailor the news feed to focus on their specific areas of interest or research, ensuring that they receive relevant and timely information.
3. **Pocket**: While not a traditional news aggregator, Pocket allows users to save articles, videos, and stories from any publication, page, or app. This is especially useful for academics who come across relevant content throughout the day but may not have the time to read it immediately. Pocket not only stores these articles but also recommends additional content based on the user's interests.

By leveraging these tools, you can efficiently curate a wealth of information, keeping informed and ready to contribute thoughtfully to your fields. This not only enhances personal knowledge but also reinforces your stature as informed and engaged experts in their respective areas of study.

the Global Association of Risk Professionals. Industry associations regularly publish research studies, industry reports, and surveys, along with newsletters and articles sharing the latest industry news and developments. Associations also keep their members abreast of the changes in regulations and policies, a critical aspect for compliance and strategic planning, as well as detailed market analyses and economic data. Regularly scanning their content opens an invaluable window into the ongoing conversations and concerns of your audience.

To ensure you are consistently updated on topics of particular interest or emerging trends, you should set up customized alerts based on specific keywords or phrases. For instance, if your expertise lies in supply chain or cryptocurrencies, setting up alerts for these terms will ensure that you receive the latest developments in those areas. This practice not only keeps you informed but also helps in synthesizing new insights.

Again, do your scanning efficiently to avoid wasting time. Think of it like picking up the morning newspaper while you have breakfast and dedicating 15 to 20 minutes daily to see what the news of the day is all about. The goal is to identify core information sources to review regularly, limiting your time and avoiding the social-media black hole. You're not reading in detail while scanning but rather looking for stories or research results that contribute to your broader understanding, advance your perspective, and are important for your community to know about. Quickly survey the news, and identify which items will require more attention at a later time.

Periodically after scanning, perhaps once a week, *select* the most relevant, high-quality content. The selection process should be based on criteria such as relevance to the field, credibility of the source, potential impact on the community, and so on. And you should also be thinking about the source's alignment with your own viewpoint on the industry. Selection is where your expertise and judgment come to the fore and is part of establishing and communicating your unique authority character and perspective to your audience.

You can use an internet note-taking app to organize your findings. Popular online note software includes Evernote, OneNote, Notion, or more academic-focused tools like Zotero or Mendeley. Spend upfront time to ensure that notes are organized in a structured manner, something that allows tagging for easy retrieval and supports multimedia and links.

As you revisit the content you've identified and find valuable, read it in more detail, and decide which pieces are worth sharing with your community. Mark these as favorites in your note-taking platform, adding notes or bullet points with your perspective.

Remember, we want to engage in *value-added* curation. That means we are not only going to select interesting content, but we are also going to tell our audience why the issue is important and what they should be thinking about it. Think about it this way: When events arise within a field, they are frequently laden with complexities and nuances that might not be immediately apparent to the broader audience. These events, whether they are breakthroughs in technology, policy changes, emerging trends, or industry challenges, form the content of your curation. However, the real value for your audience lies in the insights into the meaning and importance you see in the content. This is where you can add unique value through your perspective, opinion, and distinctive authority character.

For instance, when a new policy mandating stricter carbon reporting for corporations was released, I knew my audience would want to know about it. But simply sharing this update wouldn't suffice. My audience needed to understand its broader implications, so I provided the following context:

> "This regulation marks a pivotal shift in corporate accountability. It's no longer about ticking compliance boxes—this is a clear signal that transparency in carbon emissions will become a non-negotiable expectation. Companies that fail to integrate comprehensive carbon-reporting systems immediately risk falling behind both regulatory and market demands. For executives, the message is clear: Delay is not an option. Those who move swiftly will not only avoid penalties but will position themselves as leaders in an increasingly scrutinized business landscape. The stakes are high—this is about long-term resilience, not short-term compliance."

This approach added value by framing the content as urgent, while offering my unique perspective on what the audience should do next.

The final step is *sharing* the curated content with your audience and community. Sharing can take various forms, such as writing summary articles or blog posts, creating infographics, posting on social-media platforms, or even discussing these in lectures or webinars. The objective is to disseminate the curated content in a manner that is accessible and engaging to the target audience. Sharing also involves adding personal insights, commentary, or critique to enhance the value of the information being shared. Again, pay attention to emerging AI applications that can help you generate compelling content that previously would have required a team of designers, editors, and graphics experts.

The other important part of your value-added curation is prompting the audience to act. Academic authorities are thought leaders. That means you are leading people in how to think about, and then ultimately act on, the information and expertise you provide. Actionability is what gives run-of-the-mill information value for your audience. The goal is to spur the audience toward engagement and application of the content in their professional lives. You achieve this by suggesting practical applications, posing thought-provoking questions, or highlighting areas for further exploration. A thoughtful *call-to-action* transforms passive content consumption into active engagement. The CTA should be clear, compelling, and relevant, encouraging the audience to engage more deeply with the content. This step ensures that the content is not only understood but also utilized in a way that benefits the audience's professional growth and decision-making processes.

If you can batch your work, you can schedule selected pieces for publication on different days of the week using a *scheduling* program. Social-media scheduling tools, such as Hootsuite, Buffer, and Later, allow you to plan, schedule, and automate the posting across multiple platforms in advance. This not only saves time but also helps you maintain a steady stream of content, ensuring that you remain visible and relevant throughout the week. Features like analytics and optimal-posting-time recommendations further enhance the effectiveness of content strategy, allowing you to analyze performance and optimize your approach. By leveraging these scheduling tools, you can focus more on content curation and less on the logistics of posting, making your social-media efforts both more productive and impactful.

Ideally, you will spend a few minutes daily scanning your aggregated sources. Then, once a week, dedicate a block of time to choose the most valuable content, and add your perspective and call to action. You can then schedule your batch of posts in advance, so that your audience receives a message from you every day, even though you're actively working on this only during specific periods, such as Friday afternoons or Monday mornings. This way, you maintain a consistent presence with your audience with minimal exertion.

Curation and the Authority Trajectory

As you progress on your development trajectory, you will find that curation plays different roles at different stages. During the investment phase, curation is a tool to help you learn the conversational domain and develop your own industry synthesis, something that then forms the foundation of your unique perspective and authority character. It also helps to begin building name recognition in your chosen community.

At this stage, you will not be going terribly deep into selected content. Instead, you will primarily engage in value-added pointing through your microblog. You can also create short blog or video pieces that can follow a simple format. Begin by recognizing an important industry issue that has arisen. Next, inform your audience why it is important to them and what they should be thinking about it. Finally, tell them what they should do about the issue. This is the essence of thought leadership. You are leading people, guiding them to emergent issues, and informing them what to think about them.

An example for me was when an article about customer trust in corporate sustainability claims emerged, and I used it to point out a rising trend of greenwashing accusations in the corporate world. I began by highlighting the issue: "Greenwashing is no longer just a PR concern; it's becoming a risk for businesses as regulators and consumers become savvier about sustainability claims." I then explained why this matters: "With increasing scrutiny, even well-meaning companies can find themselves under fire if their sustainability initiatives don't align with their public messaging. The reputational and financial fallout can be severe." Here, I gave some examples of companies caught out by their questionable claims. Finally, I provided actionable advice: "Sustainability leaders should conduct rigorous internal audits of their sustainability claims and ensure they're backed by genuine evidence. Transparency and authenticity are the only ways to maintain trust and avoid damaging allegations in an increasingly skeptical world." This concise format engages the audience, informs them of the significance, and directs them on what steps to take.

While curation serves to help you master your field and establish yourself as a knowledgeable and interesting voice in the industry during the investment phase, curation takes on a different role as you move into the next step in your authority development—identifying breakthrough problems and crafting actionable solutions, the focus of the next chapter.

・・・

Added Curation Workflow

Combining news aggregators with internet note-taking software for content curation as an academic thought leader helps to create a predictable workflow. The goal is to efficiently gather, organize, and synthesize information from various sources to contribute meaningfully to your field.

Here are the steps to do this:

1. **Identify key areas and sources**:
   - Determine the main areas of interest or research within your field.
   - Identify relevant news aggregators. These could be general (like Google News) or specific to your field (like PubMed for medical research).

2. **Set up news aggregators**:
   - Customize your news-aggregator settings to follow topics, keywords, or journals that are most relevant to your academic interests.
   - Use RSS feeds to streamline information from multiple sources.

3. **Choose a note-taking tool**:
   - Select an internet note-taking software that suits your needs. Options include Evernote, OneNote, Notion, or more academic-focused tools like Zotero or Mendeley.
   - Ensure that the tool organizes notes in a structured manner, allows tagging for easy retrieval, and supports multimedia and links.

4. **Integrate news aggregators with note-taking software**:
   - Note-taking tools that allow direct integration with news aggregators or RSS feeds will automatically import articles or summaries into your notes.

5. **Organize and curate content**:
   - Create a system for organizing information in your note-taking tool (e.g., by topic, date, project, or relevance).
   - Regularly review and curate the content, highlighting key findings, adding your own insights, and making connections to your existing knowledge.

6. **Scan, select, and share:**
   - Use the information to write value-added curation messages that reflect your perspective as an academic thought leader.
   - Share your insights through your website, social media, and online communities.

7. **Review and adjust strategy**:
   - Regularly update your news-aggregator preferences as your research interests evolve.
   - Periodically review the effectiveness of your curation strategy.

Again, pay attention to developments in AI tools that are rapidly evolving and promise to streamline this further. The key to successful content curation is not just in gathering information, but in adding value through your unique perspective and insights. This process should enable you to stay at the forefront of your field and contribute meaningful dialogue and innovation.

CHAPTER 8

Crafting Solutions to Practitioner Problems

In this chapter, I focus on identifying and tackling real-world problems faced by practitioners, with an emphasis on maximizing the relevance and impact of your work. We begin by discussing the importance of choosing the right problem, as not all issues are created equal in the eyes of those who manage and lead in the business world. From there, we delve into the inductive, methodological approach employed by academic authorities to generate practical solution frameworks. These frameworks, based on observations and data collected from an authority's engagement with managers within the conversational domain, provide practitioners with actionable insights and guidance. Finally, we ensure that these solutions are validated to offer real utility to your audience.

Identifying Breakthrough Problems to Solve

The first step is identifying the problems you want to focus on. In order to create value for your community, it is essential to identify the right problems to solve. In previous chapters, we covered how engagement with managers helps develop fluency in your area and your unique synthesis of the field. Now, you'll start homing in on the variety of problems facing practitioners. Managers, you will find, confront numerous problems, not all of which hold the same potential for your work. Your challenge is choosing the right problem to study.

The focus here will be primarily on problems and solutions that might be considered appropriate for a top practitioner outlet like the *Harvard Business Review*. That said, you will also come upon important problems that you can contribute to but may not be as expansive or pressing. Richard Ettenson calls these "nagging problems." He explains: "In my work with executives, some of their challenges went back to basics or a focus on the fundamentals. The solutions I recommended were not necessarily something I could publish in *MIT Sloan*, but they were impactful nonetheless." These challenges often stem from fundamental business principles being overlooked, requiring solutions that are not necessarily groundbreaking but rather a return to core strategies, execution, and disciplined application of best practices. While we will focus here on the high-impact problems, keep in mind that there are opportunities at many levels where authorities can contribute to more niche challenges.

If you read the popular thought-leadership literature and advice for influencers, you will find authors recommending that you find your "breakthrough idea." By that, they mean a catchy concept that will distinguish you from the crowd and help you make a name for yourself. For example, professors W. Chan Kim and Renée Mauborgne of INSEAD introduced a new lexicon of competition-free market spaces, based on a simple metaphor comparing the bloody-red waters of fierce competition with potentially unexplored "blue oceans" of new market opportunity. They called their approach the Blue Ocean Strategy, publishing a popular book by the same name. Similarly, in the technological domain, we've seen ideas like Moore's Law and The Long Tail. In psychology and social sciences, we've gotten ideas like the Growth Mindset, Multiple Intelligences, and the Hierarchy of Needs. These became transformative ideas that influenced thinking and discourse for decades.

If you followed popular advice, all you would need to do is to craft and articulate your own breakthrough idea, and you'd be on your way. However, for an academic authority, this approach can be misguided. You may indeed develop a breakthrough idea, but it will stem from identifying and solving something else: a *breakthrough problem*. A breakthrough problem is a problem that, if solved, could dramatically improve organizational performance and aid practitioners in efficiently achieving their goals.

A good example of this breakthrough problem process is the MIT Future of Automobile Project led by James Womack and Daniel Jones in the 1980s. In a far-reaching endeavor, researchers and industry experts immersed themselves in an interdisciplinary analysis of the automobile industry at both the firm and global levels. They unearthed numerous problems and concerns, however, the project identified the issue of quality as a standout topic. Quality was a problem for U.S. car producers, especially during the 1960s and 1970s, as the manufacturing quality for most U.S. vehicles was abysmal in those decades.

The quality issue, if solved and broadly adopted, could dramatically improve industry performance. Through their global engagement, the researchers found that Japanese companies had been experimenting with W. Edwards Deming's theories on quality management. One company in particular, Toyota, had not only mastered Deming's quality theories but also extended the insights in innovative ways to enhance their entire production processes. The MIT study showed how Toyota had addressed and moved beyond quality to a comprehensive manufacturing solution. By exploring the methods, the project was able to explain and document their processes, which ultimately led to the breakthrough idea of Lean Manufacturing. Lean Manufacturing, inspired by the Toyota Production System, has since revolutionized global business by emphasizing waste reduction and efficiency, leading to significant cost savings and improved production quality. It has fostered a culture of continuous improvement and employee engagement, enhancing overall productivity and quality that continues to this day.

The lean case is a real example of solving breakthrough challenges. Many authorities establish successful careers without ever generating this type of breakthrough concept. However, understanding the process of those that do can help guide your work at any level. So, as you engage with practitioners and begin discovering their problems, you will be evaluating the potential impact resolving an issue might have. A useful way to categorize the problems you encounter, and solutions you can deliver, has been elaborated by Dartmouth

Tuck School's Vijay Govindarajan. Govindarajan notes that there are basically three classes of problem solutions, which are illustrated in the graphic below. The key differentiator is the potential impact that resolving a problem could have for practitioners and industry.

Choose the Right Problem

Academics	Consultants	Authorities
"COMMON" Practice	"BEST" Practice	"NEXT" Practice
$N=10^x$	$N=10x$	$N=1$

LOW ──────────────▶ HIGH
POTENTIAL IMPACT ON BUSINESS

At the left of the spectrum are *common-practice* problems. These are long-standing issues that have been the historic focus of academic research and for which there are many examples and studies. These are good problems for academic research because, for statistically significant research results, a large sample size is required. However, a large sample population usually means the issue is widespread and well known. Most academic research here would involve testing the validity of known theory in novel populations or some other incremental advance of existing theory. Common-practice research is typical of the academic approach that seeks statistical rigor. "If you're an empirical researcher, you're doing common practice," Govindarajan explains. "You collect data from a thousand companies, set up an hypothesis, and say that thousands of companies are doing it. That research doesn't produce any impact. You're essentially telling me what everyone is already doing."

A good example of a common-practice problem is the long-standing issue of employee-performance-appraisal systems. Most organizations use annual performance reviews to assess employee contributions, set goals, and determine raises or promotions. This process is deeply ingrained in corporate human-research management and is widespread, making it a reliable subject for research due to the large sample sizes available for study. Numerous academic theories, such as goal-setting theory and expectancy theory, have already explored and refined best practices in this area. However, while performance appraisals remain central to organizational processes, studying them often results in incremental theoretical advancements rather than offering breakthrough solutions, which is why they fall under the category of common-practice problems.

While valid academic contributions to the discipline, common-practice problems do not portend a major impact on business practice and performance.

In the middle of the spectrum, Govindarajan recognizes something he calls *best-practice* problems. In contrast to common practice, these are recently understood problems for which best practices are currently employed by perhaps a third of companies. If properly researched and systematized, best-practice solutions could potentially impact the remaining two-thirds of the sector that have not adopted the approach. Best-practice solutions can offer a big contribution to practice, and, because of the potential impact on companies, they are often seen as a market and business opportunity. This tends to draw in consulting firms that repackage and spread best-practice solutions to their clients.

Over the decades, we have seen many ideas become "best-practice" business fads aimed at enhancing organizational performance and competitiveness. In the 1970s, for example, the concept of Management by Objectives (MBO), which emphasized setting clear, measurable goals that are agreed upon by both management and employees, gained substantial traction. In the 1980s, we saw the rise of Total Quality Management (TQM), initially focusing on continuous quality improvement and eventually evolving to encompass everything from company culture to manufacturing processes. During the 1990s, Business Process Re-engineering (BPR) emerged as an approach to achieving significant improvements in productivity, cycle times, and quality. During the 2000s, the concept of Corporate Social Responsibility (CSR) came to the forefront, encouraging companies to make a positive impact on society while enhancing their brand and bottom line. Today the focus has shifted toward

ACADEMIC AUTHORITY

Digital Transformation, embracing business applications of new technologies such as cloud computing, big data analytics, and artificial intelligence.

As an academic thought leader, you will find opportunities to contribute to corporate best practices, sometimes in the context of a consulting engagement. Companies will often have resources and access to substantial data that will allow you to utilize traditional research methodologies. Texas Tech Distinguished Professor James Wetherbe has written about some of his thought-leadership work in this vein. In one instance, while serving on Best Buy's board of directors, Wetherbe received a $500,000 grant to lead a research team exploring the behavior of the company's online shoppers. The team's work, using company data, showed that shipping costs were deterring potential buyers, leading to abandoned carts. Based on this insight, Best Buy began offering free shipping for online purchases, significantly boosting their sales. As stated, many companies will have these types of issues, and they can represent enticing consulting opportunities for entrepreneurial academics interested in this type of best-practice work. This is where you can also find "nagging problems" for which academic research and theory has something to say, if the authority can articulate it in a way that catches managerial attention and guides them in implementing it.

While spreading best practice is consequential for business performance, Govindarajan recommends another type of problem and solution for academic thought leaders wishing to have a big impact on practice. He calls these *next-practice* solutions, which are pioneering approaches to resolving emergent management issues. Because they are new problems, perhaps only a handful of companies are actively working to tackle them. By discovering these issues, understanding their nature, and examining the various efforts executives are using to solve them, academic authorities can help push the frontier of management. By systematizing and providing guidance on how to resolve these emergent challenges, authorities can have an outsized impact on industry performance.

An example of an academic authority providing a next-practice solution is Michael Porter's concept of Creating Shared Value (CSV). In the early 2010s, Porter recognized that Corporate Social Responsibility was often treated as a peripheral activity, disconnected from core business strategies. Porter's solution, introduced in his 2011 *Harvard Business Review* article, redefined the role of business in society by proposing that companies could create economic value by addressing social and environmental challenges as part of their core operations. Unlike traditional CSR, Porter's shared-value framework positioned societal problems as opportunities for business innovation and competitive advantage. Pioneering companies, like Nestlé, were pursuing shared value to improve water management, rural development, and nutrition, generating both social impact and financial returns. By naming and explaining the phenomenon, Porter has since influenced broader corporate-sustainability strategies, making it a classic example of a next-practice solution that anticipated future business needs.

Another example of a next-practice solution is Tom Davenport's pioneering work on big data analytics and artificial intelligence in business decision-making, well before the current AI boom began. In his 2013 book, *Big Data at Work*, Davenport recognized the transformative potential of using big data and AI to drive business strategies, moving beyond traditional, intuition-based decision-making. At the time, only a few companies were experimenting with data-driven approaches, making this a next-practice problem. Davenport's framework guided early adopters, such as GE and UPS, in using predictive analytics to optimize critical operations like supply-chain management and predictive maintenance. His work has since become foundational as more businesses embrace AI to navigate a data-driven future, illustrating how next-practice solutions can anticipate the broader adoption of emerging technologies.

Despite the potential impact, next-practice solutions create a conundrum for academics. Many rigorous statistical-research methods require large N sample populations. But large N groups are, almost by definition, common practices because there are many examples, and the concern is already ubiquitous. While useful for statistical rigor, these problems offer limited potential impact for practitioners. Next practices, by contrast, involve smaller N populations. But while small N populations may not be acceptable for statistical analysis, that doesn't mean an investigation cannot be pursued rigorously. While there are dangers of overgeneralizing from a small sample, delving deeply into a single company or small number of companies provides a viable path for discovering practices that could advance management practice.

We need to think differently about these problems and what we are trying to achieve. Unlike common-practice issues, where hypotheses are tested, next-practice problems involve generating hypotheses and elaborating theory. As Govindarajan explains: "Whereas the focus of common-practice research is hypothesis testing, the focus of next-practice research is hypothesis generation." The goal is to generate grounded and field-validated solution hypotheses that managers can use to guide their understanding of the problem and the decision factors they need to consider when addressing them. And, of course, this requires employing research methodologies suited to investigating emergent concerns with limited data.

To identify breakthrough problems, you need to engage with your community. You will also benefit by looking for a specific type of manager to work with. As discussed, you will quickly find that not all managers are the same. USC's Ann Majchrzak seeks out *reflective practitioners* that are thinking about their future. Wharton's George Day calls this second group *thoughtful practitioners,* saying: "I find that, by working with really thoughtful managers, you get deep insights into problems that managers are facing."

These managers can be frustrated intellectuals who may have wanted to work in academia but fell into business instead and enjoy thinking carefully about their work and discussing trends with other people. These managers are exceptionally valuable to an academic authority. By identifying and cultivating productive relationships with thoughtful managers, you can gain beneficial insights into both emerging breakthrough problems and potential solutions. You need to discriminate carefully here. You will find that managers are happy to take free consulting from you while having little to contribute that can help advance your work. Do your best due diligence to find thoughtful executives that can offer mutually productive engagements with you.

You'll typically discover breakthrough problems in the areas of an organization that are struggling with questions like: "*What are the bottlenecks? What are the areas where resources are not being utilized efficiently? What are the pain points for customers or employees?*" Areas that are experiencing rapid growth

Investigation with Limited Data

For emergent concerns that lack substantial historical data, different methods can be applied. The approach shifts from deductive toward inductive methods, with a focus on elaborating grounded hypotheses that generate, rather than test, theory.

Grounded theory involves the simultaneous collection of data and development of theory. Through interviews, observations, or case studies, investigators can gather rich qualitative data, which informs the creation of theories tailored to the specific problem. The approach is usually inductive, developing more generalized theories from specific observations.

Theory-building techniques, such as *analogical reasoning*, *interdisciplinary approaches*, and *systems thinking* are also often beneficial. Analogical reasoning allows you to draw parallels to the immediate concern with better-understood phenomena. Both systems thinking and interdisciplinary methods can draw from various fields to provide a multifaceted understanding of complex issues, including novel managerial problems. By integrating perspectives, theories, and tools from disciplines, interdisciplinary approaches can offer more comprehensive insights into managerial challenges that are often too complex for a single-discipline perspective.

By employing these techniques, academic thought leaders can make contributions to understanding emergent problems in the face of limited data. These evidence-based approaches can also create a theoretical foundation that can guide further research and practical action in newly emerging fields.

or change also tend to be rich with challenges, as organizations struggle to keep up with shifting demand, technologies, policies, economics, and the like. Ettenson's nagging problems—those that are not being addressed or that are being addressed but not solved effectively—are golden. Listen carefully to the responses you get from managers, and ask follow-up questions to deepen your understanding of their needs.

Recently, while interviewing sustainability managers as part of an *MIT SMR* project, I uncovered a breakthrough problem related to capturing the intangible value of sustainability efforts. During this engagement, it became clear that, while sustainability initiatives generate significant value for companies—particularly with key stakeholders like millennial employees, customers, and investors—much of this value was intangible and difficult to measure. Millennial employees, for example, were rewarding companies they perceived as responsible with loyalty and engagement, while customers tended to favor brands that were committed to environmental and social causes. However, it was challenging to demonstrate causal connections. Increased stakeholder goodwill didn't easily translate into communicable financial outcomes. The breakthrough problem was clear: How can companies "tangibilize" these intangible benefits to capture their full value and enhance long-term business success?

Through the work with executives, I explored approaches to making intangible sustainability impacts more tangible to stakeholders. This culminated in a 2024 *Harvard Business Review* article where I outlined the methods companies can use to make intangible sustainability benefits more visible and thus more valuable. Addressing this breakthrough problem helped companies position their sustainability efforts as profitable long-term strategies, not just temporary subsidies—an important shift for business sustainability.

As in this example, the discovery of potential solutions to your chosen problem usually comes through your direct engagement in the conversational domain of managers. As Day explained: "You're not looking back and collecting data and trying to prove a theory; you're actually framing emergent problems. . . . it's an immersive process." Davenport concurred: "Your research methods have to be different as well. You have to look sort of anthropologically innocent at what's happening and get a better understanding of it by observation." The graphic below illustrates the discovery process described by the academic authorities interviewed in this book.

As the figure illustrates, by conversing with managers in their conversational domain, you collect data about the chosen problem, and, as your discussions

Discover a Solution

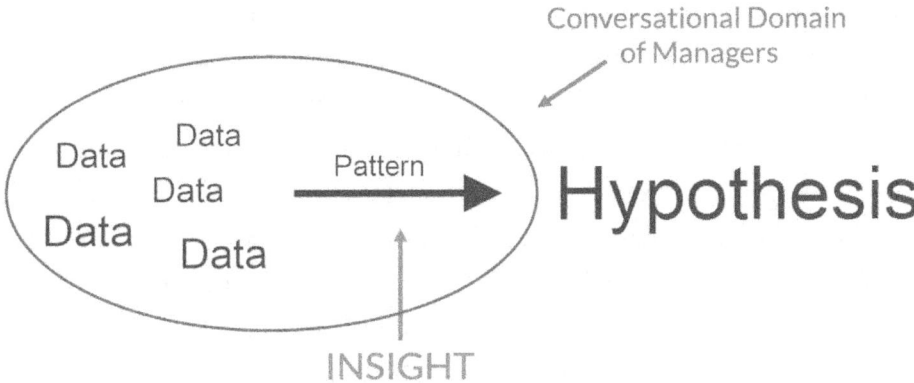

continue, patterns begin to emerge. You can then begin to draw inductive insights from the observed patterns. Often, the discovery comes in a flash of insight. Andrew Campbell described it colorfully: "It's like the rabbit's tail. It's a glimpse. A rabbit's tail is white, and, when it disappears down a hole, you see that little flash of white. It's a glimpse of what might be interesting."

The rabbit's tail insight marks the transition from observation to hypothesis formulation. Having identified where you see a potential resolution to the problem, you begin a process of simplifying and then systematize a solution for it. You'll develop an hypothesis for how the problem can be solved, which serves as the basis for your eventual solution framework.

When working with practitioners, you'll often find they are absorbed in the immediate challenges of their roles, dealing directly with problems as they arise. In a fast-paced business environment, the pressure to deliver on operational tasks leaves little room for stepping back to look at the broader picture. Managers typically rely on trial and error and learning by doing, often solving problems instinctively rather than systematically. As Ettenson notes: "They often prefer the quick fix regardless of whether it is an enduring solution." The manager's form of implicit learning provides an opportunity for an academic authority to step in. While practitioners are focused on immediate solutions, they often miss opportunities for structured, strategic insights, and this is where the academic can add immense value.

ACADEMIC AUTHORITY

Because they rarely have the time to formally document the processes they use, their solutions remain tacit and unarticulated. An academic authority, however, has both the perspective and the capacity to investigate these implicit understandings and convert them into explicit, replicable knowledge. By analyzing, refining, and codifying the unspoken strategies practitioners employ, you can transform emergent practices into formalized guidance that others can adopt. This ability to extract, organize, and systematize knowledge not only helps solve the immediate problem but also equips the broader community of business leaders with tools and frameworks that can be applied in similar contexts. Ultimately, this is where your unique contribution as an academic lies—taking what is emergent and making it teachable, scalable, and actionable for others. Your ability to simplify for managers can be incredibly valuable.

As you navigate the research process, you will encounter three distinct types of knowledge that are important for solving breakthrough problems. Understanding and recognizing these forms of knowledge—explicit, implicit, and tacit knowledge—will enable you to extract the most relevant insights needed to develop comprehensive solutions. *Explicit knowledge* is readily available and easily articulated. Found in written guides, procedures, and documented systems, it can be directly accessed through interviews or existing resources, providing a clear foundation for your research. In contrast, *implicit knowledge* is embedded within a company's culture and practices. It manifests in the unwritten rules or behaviors that managers rely on, often revealed through observation and skilled questioning. This knowledge is crucial for understanding how things get done in practice, even if they aren't formally documented. Finally, *tacit knowledge* is the most complex and personal form—it resides in individual experiences, instincts, and intuitions. Often shared through stories or personal anecdotes in interviews, tacit knowledge provides deep insights into a manager's problem-solving approach that might not be consciously articulated.

Your approach is akin to that of a coach analyzing an athlete's golf swing. Why does a golfer need a coach? Because they can't see their own swing. That is, they cannot get an objective perspective on what it is they are doing correctly or wrong. The coach first observes the player in action, paying close attention to their technique—evaluating elements such as posture, timing,

Types of Knowledge

When extracting solutions, it helps to distinguish between **explicit**, **implicit**, and **tacit knowledge**, as each plays a different role in how practitioners learn and apply solutions:

- **Explicit knowledge**: This is the most easily communicated form of knowledge, as it's formal, structured, and systematically documented. Explicit knowledge can be found in training manuals, operating procedures, databases, practitioner publications, and academic papers. It is straightforward to share among individuals and across organizations because it's codified and universally accessible.

- **Implicit knowledge**: While not formally documented, implicit knowledge emerges through practice and experience. It involves skills or competencies that are passed on through mentorship, observation, or repetition, without being fully articulated.

- **Tacit knowledge**: The most elusive and personal form of knowledge, tacit knowledge is deeply rooted in individual experience and specific contexts. It is often subconscious and difficult to express or document because it includes personal insights, intuitions, and hunches. Tacit knowledge can involve everything from gut feelings about a market shift to nuanced understandings of team dynamics, making it challenging to formalize or transfer.

and grip. Through this detailed analysis, the coach identifies specific areas where the player's form breaks down, whether it's a misaligned stance or poor follow-through. Once these issues are understood, the coach dissects the problem, breaking it into manageable pieces, and isolates the critical areas for improvement. This step-by-step diagnosis helps to clarify what needs adjustment and why.

Similarly, after analyzing a practitioner's approach to problem-solving, you can identify the strengths and weaknesses in their methods. Once the issues are clear, you provide structured solution steps, much like a coach offering practical advice for improvement. By breaking down their implicit processes into explicit, actionable strategies, you help practitioners turn instinctive approaches into systematic methods that can be applied consistently. Your role is to translate their experience into a clear framework that enhances their decision-making and execution.

Your engagement with thoughtful and reflective managers is key to this process. By observing, tweaking, and sometimes offering recommendations, you work with managers currently facing these problems to systematize and simplify the solution. Your role involves diving into the trenches with them, understanding the problem from their perspective, and formulating an articulated, replicable, and explicit solution. You're tasked with making this solution explicit, systematizing it into a teachable form. Most often this will take the form of a conceptual solution framework.

In my example above, I discovered the challenge of capturing the intangible value of sustainability efforts while working with sustainability managers. The problem was that, while companies could recognize the benefits of sustainability initiatives, the benefits were difficult to measure and communicate to stakeholders. To address this, I articulated a solution that focused on "tangibilizing" intangible benefits through three basic strategies, including storytelling, third-party validation, and transparency. This then became a simple framework that helped businesses capture intangible sustainability value, ensuring the efforts were sustained as "just good business."

Crafting Your Solution Framework

After explicitly articulating a solution to the breakthrough problem, you are now at the point where you can begin to structure your solution. Crafting the solution is both a science and an art. It's crucial to structure the solution in a way that is useful and interesting for managers. This is typically done through actionable solution frameworks.

Actionable solution frameworks are common in management fields and provide practitioners with structured approaches to tackle complex challenges, guide decision-making, and strategize effectively. The Balanced Scorecard, for example, developed by HBS professors Robert Kaplan and David Norton, is a management framework that helps managers translate their vision and strategy into a coherent set of performance metrics. And the SWOT Analysis (Strengths, Weaknesses, Opportunities, Threats), which is ubiquitous in strategy textbooks, provides a simple framework for assessing an organization's internal and external environment to inform strategy development.

Business schools teach many frameworks like the PESTEL analysis (external macro-environmental factors) from Francis Aguilar, the Value Chain analysis (operations management) from Michael Porter, the Ansoff Matrix (marketing and strategic planning) from Igor Ansoff, and the VRIO Framework (resource-based view of the firm) from Jay Barney. These frameworks highlight the key aspects of a problem, breaking them down into manageable components for analysis and decision-making.

Frameworks are a quintessential thought-leadership tool because they are literally designed to structure a manager's thinking about a specific problem. For example, in the diamond industry, jewelers must determine a diamond's value, which isn't immediately quantifiable and involves judgment. In order to structure their thinking about what makes a diamond valuable, jewelers use the Four Cs of Diamonds to provide a framework for judging and pricing their diamonds. The Four Cs include carat weight, color grade, clarity grade, and cut grade. This framework serves as a map or blueprint of the key decision factors that is easily remembered, allowing it to be internalized and used without referring back to a detailed manual.

Michael Porter's Five Forces framework is a prime example that effectively meets several of the criteria in the box "Key Features of a Well-Crafted Framework." It contextualizes thinking by placing a firm within the broader landscape of its industry's competitive forces, allowing strategists to appreciate the complexities of their market environment. By organizing thinking, the

Key Features of a Well-Crafted Framework

A strong framework transforms complex challenges into clear, actionable strategies. Here are the essential features of an effective framework:

- **Offers clarity of purpose**: Clearly defines the overarching goal of the framework, ensuring all processes and actions align with the desired outcome.

- **Contextualizes the problem**: Situates the issue within a broader business system, helping stakeholders understand the larger context and its implications.

- **Organizes complex information**: Breaks down intricate data or concepts, often using visual aids, to make the information more manageable and easier to interpret.

- **Highlights key elements**: Draws attention to the most critical factors that need focus, ensuring that resources and energy are directed toward the most impactful areas.

- **Provides criteria for comparison**: Establishes benchmarks or standards that allow for evaluation of different options or strategies, making it easier to assess performance or outcomes.

- **Elucidates causal implications**: Reveals how specific actions or decisions can lead to particular outcomes, giving decision-makers a clearer understanding of cause-and-effect relationships.

- **Outlines processes or steps**: Offers a systematic, step-by-step approach for tackling the problem, guiding managers through the implementation process in a structured way.

- **Is adaptable**: Allows flexibility so the framework can be customized to fit different contexts or challenges.

- **Is easy to communicate**: Simple enough to explain and implement across various teams and stakeholders, ensuring widespread understanding and application.

framework segments the competitive landscape into five distinct forces. This categorization highlights the key strategy elements, focusing attention on the most significant aspects of competition. The framework also provides criteria for comparison, enabling firms to evaluate their position relative to these forces and benchmark against competitors. Additionally, it implicitly shows causal implications by suggesting how changes in any of the forces could affect the competitive dynamics and, consequently, the firm's strategic choices. Finally, while Porter's framework does not prescribe a specific step-by-step process, it guides the strategic-analysis process, prompting firms to systematically assess each force, thereby informing their strategic decisions to enhance competitiveness and profitability.

While developing a solution framework requires a blend of creativity and methodical structure, there are some clear steps you can follow to transform your insights into a structured, actionable model. Start by identifying the core components that capture the essence of the managerial problem and its potential solutions. These components could range from specific behaviors and practices to broader processes and organizational dynamics observed during your study. Once identified, map out how these components interact within the managerial ecosystem, highlighting causal relationships, dependencies, and feedback loops that influence outcomes. This level of analysis helps ensure that the framework reflects the complexity and nuances of real-world management scenarios.

Five Forces Framework

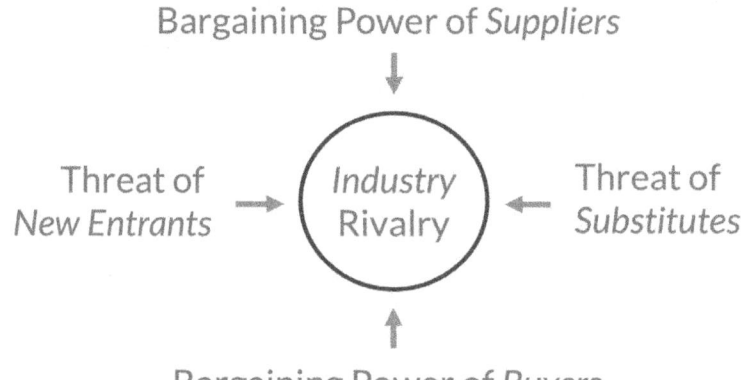

A well-crafted framework doesn't stop at diagnosis; it can also outline key processes and actions that managers can take to address the problem. These processes should be logically sequenced and rooted in best practices, ensuring that the strategies are both actionable and effective. Flexibility is key here—the framework should be adaptable to different organizational contexts, allowing managers to tailor the solution to their specific challenges.

One of the most important elements of a framework is implementation guidelines, such as step-by-step instructions, diagnostic tools, or templates that make it easy for managers to apply. The internal consistency of the framework should be carefully verified, ensuring that all components and recommendations work together harmoniously and are free from contradictions.

Crucially, a robust framework is designed with an eye toward iterative refinement. Given the dynamic nature of managerial challenges, the framework should include mechanisms for collecting feedback on its application and effectiveness. This feedback loop ensures the framework remains a living document, continuously evolving and improving based on real-world experiences. Recognizing that no framework is static, the iterative process underscores the importance of creating a solution that is not only grounded in empirical insights but also adaptable to new challenges and responsive to feedback.

Your goal should be to create a framework that is teachable by mapping out the key variables and their relationships within the context of the problem. This approach allows you to visually organize and illustrate how different elements interact. However, you should keep in mind that it is an hypothesis that needs validation. Your framework is ultimately a solution hypothesis. Its true value lies in real-world applicability.

Again, some of your work might discover problems and solutions that will not find their way onto the pages of *HBR*. That does not mean they are not valuable. "I have 20+ 'homegrown' frameworks," explains Ettenson, "that will never make it into a publication. But they provide the foundations for most of my classroom teaching, whether MBAs or Executives." Many of your frameworks can serve your teaching, or they might find their way into more sector-specific industry association journals, such as *IndustryWeek, Food & Business News*, and *Oil & Gas Investor*.

Validate Your Framework

There are two primary ways you validate your framework. First is to rely on your academic training. You should use your academic expertise by rigorously applying disciplinary knowledge to assess the framework's effectiveness. Your framework should align with what is known in the academic literature. Collaboration with your academic peers is useful for refining frameworks and ensuring their rigor. Your peers can provide a critical academic perspective and testing against disciplinary understandings.

However, the real value and validity of your framework comes largely from the managers that will be using it. Its value depends on the utility it provides practicing managers. This is one of the big disconnects between most academic research and practice in business schools. We don't usually develop and test our theories through engagement with practicing professionals. An

HBR editor once told me about an interesting anecdote on this point. He said he'd met an academic who presented an interesting framework and approach. The editor inquired about its practical application, to which the academic replied that it hadn't been used yet. He had basically created the theoretical ideas in his head while sitting in his faculty office. The editor's advice was straightforward: "Go out and have someone use it. It looks interesting, but we don't know if it works or not, since it's not validated." In a rare case, the professor actually followed the editor's advice. He went out and collaborated with some companies to apply the framework successfully. The companies were pleased, and their application of the framework created a series of case demonstrations. The professor used the experience to refine his framework and craft a compelling manuscript that he shared with the editor. This then led to a highly popular *HBR* article and substantial attention for the professor. By grounding frameworks in practical application rather than letting them remain mere flights of imagination, we demonstrate their utility for managers.

There are many ways academic authorities show the utility of their frameworks. As Andrew Campbell explains: "Your whole research is about talking to managers and communicating with managers. . . . You're feeding back what you've learned to them." And in so doing, you test and refine the hypothesis. This can be done by reaching out to your network of professionals and sharing your work. Sometimes they will invite you to present your work to their companies' managers. Here you can get feedback on the practicality and utility of the framework in the eyes of the managers and make refinements to your approach. The exciting part is when you present your findings to them, and managers recognize the utility of your interpretation. It is very rewarding when executives validate your work, saying things like, "Yeah, that's what is happening. I never would have thought to spell it out that way but, yes, that's how it works."

In one instance, I generated what I called the Sustainability Triage Framework through interviews with managers who were grappling with a wide range of sustainability issues, trying to determine which of these were truly strategic for their businesses. The framework emerged as a way to help companies quickly assess whether a particular sustainability issue was merely a market expectation or an opportunity to gain a competitive advantage. I subsequently validated the framework by applying it to specific issues facing actual companies. PepsiCo, for example, recognized packaging waste was a strategic sustainability issue, largely because discarded snack bags become branded litter. Real-world applications like this showed the framework's effectiveness and, at a sustainability conference where I presented the work, I found managers approaching me to share how the framework had clarified their own challenges, helping them see them in a new light.

For those fortunate enough to teach in executive MBA programs or executive-education programs, introducing frameworks directly into the classroom offers a prime opportunity to vet with managers and refine the framework. Feedback from executives, who may challenge and push back on the framework, enables its refinement. Many of the academic thought leaders I interviewed described how their executive audiences served as a type of laboratory for elaborating, refining, and validating their ideas and frameworks. Some even used the audience for data collection, having participants fill out structured questionnaires.

This dual validation process—ensuring utility for managers and soundness within academic theory—is key. However, even though your framework resonates with practicing managers, you need to remember that it is still a grounded solution hypothesis, and you should be constantly open to ongoing iterative refinements. Think of your framework as a provisional map, providing a compass for executives traveling in a new and unfamiliar managerial terrain. It is based on your best insights up until this point. But as your framework gains traction, more managers will use it, giving you renewed opportunities to test its utilities and refine it. It is an ongoing process of updating and refining theories as new data become available. This approach ensures that your theoretical framework remains relevant and accurately reflects the evolving understanding of the problem.

• • •

CHAPTER 9

Communicating Your Solutions

Now that you have developed your solutions frameworks, you need to effectively communicate your insights to your audience. In this chapter, I will show you how to do so with authority.

This communication process begins initially by moving your content to other people's platforms. You have identified communities, such as industry associations, where your target audience congregates. Accessing these organizational platforms allows you to communicate your message to your audience. In Chapter 7, we introduced the different value-adding formats, such as articles, podcasts, videos, and blogs. Here I will explore how these formats can complement your content and demonstrate your unique perspective and authority character. Finally, I will cover high-impact practitioner outlets, like *Harvard Business Review* and the *MIT Sloan Management Review*.

I will first focus on delivering free content, through which you build visibility and recognition of your expertise. By creating value for people, you cultivate an audience of community members who are interested in what you have to say. Once you have a dedicated audience, the potential to be compensated for your content also rises. For those of you curious about this, we will discuss this in Part III.

ACADEMIC AUTHORITY

Sharing Your Insights

You have been building your audience through your value-added curation. You've discovered community problems, extracted solutions, and crafted frameworks that address the concerns. Communicating your solutions becomes a natural extension of this process. Your engagement and work with managers will have prepared you to write in a way that resonates with your audience.

"When you're feeding back what you've learned to managers, you're learning to speak their language. So, it's then relatively easy to write up a good article because you've probably been teaching it in class," says Andrew Campbell. "You've been talking to managers and interacting. You have dozens of examples to draw on. It is natural to you." Of course, you will be using the conversational domain of your audience while presenting your frameworks and compelling examples.

As Campbell indicates, in developing your communication skills, you have an invaluable laboratory for testing your frameworks and refining your communication style: *your university classroom*. The classroom environment offers an opportunity to engage directly with a bestowed audience that mirrors the diverse backgrounds and perspectives of the broader business community. This setting allows you to experiment with and hone your approach to communicating your concepts and solutions, testing your frameworks in real time, gathering feedback, and adjusting them as necessary.

The classroom allows for an iterative process of building out your solutions presentation to your community. You apply and test frameworks in real time with managers, receiving immediate feedback from students who are often practitioners themselves. This dynamic interaction facilitates a deeper understanding of the practical implications of your frameworks and enables you to refine your communication strategies.

Creating your own specialized elective offers a valuable vehicle to advance your work and ideas. By designing a course that focuses on your area of specialization and explores the cutting-edge topics you are discovering in your field, you can help students better understand real-world business challenges while advancing your ability to communicate your understanding. The elective format provides the flexibility to experiment with innovative teaching methods, incorporate the latest industry trends, and tailor content to reflect the evolving landscape of business practice. It also helps solidify your synthesis of the field.

For several years, I co-taught a course on global leadership, where we invited many global executives as guest speakers. These visits allowed us not only to engage with top leadership but also to conduct interviews and build lasting relationships with these executives. For several of the executives, we developed case studies to explore their situations and challenges with our class. The insights gained from these interactions formed the basis of an article focusing on global leadership, published in *Harvard Business Review*. The work eventually evolved into a full book-length treatment published by Harvard Business Press, helping solidify our position in the field of global leadership. The manuscript was also seen as an important marketing vehicle for the university, which was positioned as a leader in global management. The school not only distributed copies of the book to its various constituencies but also arranged a substantial public relations campaign that amplified the book's impact with practitioners.

As the example illustrates, creating and utilizing your own case studies and teaching examples gives life to your framework concepts, making them relatable and tangible for students. These cases not only enrich the classroom experience but also serve as original content for articles, publications, and speeches, extending the reach of your thought leadership. As you engage with managers, you will find many opportunities to develop interesting studies that allow you to explore breakthrough problems. You can also use cases from the institutional case libraries to enrich your curriculum and understanding, exposing you and your students to a variety of perspectives and approaches within the field. I often find that interpreting cases developed by other authors through the lens of my solution frameworks provides great opportunities to broaden the application of the framework and also test its validity against new case data in front of an audience of manager students.

Early in my career, for example, I was part of a consortium led by Harvard Business School that funded a series of case studies on sustainable business initiatives. The consortium included companies from a range of industries partnering with professors to write the cases. I found that teaching all of these cases accelerated my synthesis of the emerging field. With the diverse real-world examples, I was able to develop a breadth of expertise across multiple sustainability contexts, from procurement to corporate governance. This exposure helped me craft my unique perspective on the evolving conversation about corporate sustainability. This is a point that Rich Ettenson also makes. What is common practice in one industry or sector is not always so in another. This opens opportunities to extend your expertise in one area to new industries and geographies and expand your authority reach.

You can also generate opportunities to engage directly with managers through corporate visits during which you share your work. As you network and engage with managers, be on the lookout for these types of opportunities. I once met a group of Intel managers and arranged a visit to their headquarters, where I interviewed executives about their corporate-responsibility initiatives. This engagement not only deepened my understanding of how a major tech company was grappling with sustainability challenges but also led to the development of a case study on Intel's approach. The insights from these conversations became part of my presentations at industry conferences and content for my *Forbes* column.

Ideally, as discussed, you will want to move up in the hierarchy of seniority in your teaching. Ascending from undergraduates to MBAs, to EMBAs, and ultimately to the executive level, if possible, is a powerful way to put you in direct engagement with the managers you want to reach. As you progress, the complexity of the challenges, issues, and concerns presented by your audience increases, offering a richer foundation for developing and testing your solutions. Engaging with a more senior audience not only sharpens your communication skills but also deepens your understanding of the nuances and subtleties involved in executive decision-making and strategy formulation.

Your classroom, therefore, is not just a space to transfer received knowledge but a crucible for developing your skills and ideas that address and advance the present-day problems facing managers. By using the classroom as a laboratory, you can significantly enhance your ability to communicate complex ideas effectively and establish yourself as an authoritative voice in your field.

I have used my sustainable business elective throughout my academic career as a space to explore emergent issues, develop my solution frameworks, and refine and validate them with MBAs and executives. As previously mentioned, I launched my authority trajectory primarily because my students wanted straightforward frameworks for thinking through sustainability issues, and none were available. Over time I have developed an entire suite of teaching materials, including a textbook, cases, assignments, and videos. I also found my university had a need for other faculty members who could teach business sustainability, so I created a website of faculty resources as a turnkey way for other professors to adopt my course approach. It is similar to how textbook publishers provide a teaching guide, test bank, and other materials to faculty adopting their textbook. Today, professors in many parts of the world are using my materials and teaching frameworks in their courses, something that any academic authority should consider as a goal of their practitioner work.

Communication as Part of Your Development Trajectory

The way you communicate, and the channels you use, will evolve as you move along your authority-development trajectory. Many academic authorities aspire to immediately contribute to high-impact practitioner journals like *Harvard Business Review* or *MIT Sloan Management Review*. While this can happen, doing so right out of the gate is not typical. Think of the process as akin to breaking into the big leagues. Initially, you may not have a feel for these journals, and you may lack the kind of reputation that facilitates access for you to pitch your ideas. You normally have to build up to it. Formula One drivers don't start behind the wheel of a $15 million race car. They work their way up from lower-tier circuits, beginning with karting and progressing through Formula Four, Three, and Two before breaking into Formula One.

In your trajectory, consider three circuit levels. Initially you will use your own platform, including your website and chosen social media, for your value-added curation. From there, you focus on communicating with your target audience through the established professional channels and industry associations where they already congregate. These channels can be very productive, and many academic authorities spend the majority of their career communicating through industry media outlets alone. At the peak circuit level are the high-impact practitioner journals like *HBR* and *MIT SMR*.

Besides the communication-channel hierarchy, there are also varying formats to consider. As discussed, the primary medium you choose depends on your style. If you enjoy speaking, podcasts might be more appealing. Conversely, if you prefer writing, you might focus more on articles and blogs. Ideally, you'll engage in a combination of these methods to build out your platform.

As you create your solution frameworks, you can begin sharing them through your platform, refining your ability to communicate with practitioners

Your Own Platform

In the early stages of your trajectory, you are engaging in value-added curation, developing your industry synthesis, and establishing your unique perspective and authority character. At the beginning, you will start with outlets you can control, including your own website, podcast, blog, or video channel. You will also use social media to build out your content, writing articles on LinkedIn or utilizing platforms like Medium for longer-format articles.

As discussed, the combination of your authority website and social-media accounts creates a syndication system for your content, amplifying its reach and impact. Your website serves as the core of your digital presence—a controlled space where your insights, achievements, and solutions are presented. Meanwhile, social media acts like a syndication engine, driving traffic to your website and enabling engagement with your audience. This system promotes your content across platforms, building momentum for your thought leadership.

in compelling ways. You are building out a portfolio of content that exemplifies your perspective and character. Ideally, you will want a mix of articles by you as well as audio recordings and videos of you speaking authoritatively.

At the investment phase of your trajectory, along with your articles and online content, you can look for opportunities to develop your skills as a public speaker and presenter. In the speaking world, there is something known as the "Rubber Chicken Circuit," which are speaking engagements at banquets, luncheons, and dinners hosted by various civic, business, and charitable organizations. The name refers to the stereotypically overcooked chicken often served at these events. For speakers building their reputations, if used correctly, the Rubber Chicken Circuit can be a valuable platform. It offers a chance to hone your public-speaking skills, test your ideas in front of diverse audiences, and increase your visibility. Navigating this circuit has historically been a rite of passage for aspiring public speakers, providing essential practice in communication and engagement that can pave the way to more prestigious speaking engagements and opportunities for influence.

To find speaking opportunities, network within your local community, civic, and business circles. Start by identifying your community organizations that regularly host events, like the Rotary Club, Chamber of Commerce, service clubs, professional associations, and charitable groups. These organizations often seek guest speakers and are usually enthusiastic about having university professors keynote their events. Networking at association events and engaging directly with members can open doors to speaking invitations. Additionally, leveraging online platforms like LinkedIn to connect with organization leaders or event coordinators can be effective. It is important to remember that these groups are usually not your ultimate target audience, as they are a mix of different members from the community. By testing your presentations and developing your skills, you will be in top form by the time you are in front of your target audience and community.

As a graduate student, my advisor couldn't make a presentation on climate change to a group of local businessmen, and asked me to fill in. I was nervous, knowing the audience would be skeptical, and as expected, they hit me with tough questions, challenging the relevance of climate

Help for Novice Speakers

For those beginning a speaking journey, joining an organization like Toastmasters International can be useful. This organization teaches public-speaking skills through a global network of clubs, offering both in-person and online meetings. It provides a structured, supportive environment to develop and refine both prepared and impromptu speaking abilities. If you are seeking to overcome anxiety, polish your skills, or gain practice, this organization can be a resource.

Many prominent speakers began their journeys with Toastmasters. The author, coach, and motivational speaker Tony Robbins, for example, participated in three different Toastmasters clubs simultaneously early in his career and credits the experience with helping him develop his dynamic speaking style. Toastmasters International honored Robbins with the Golden Gavel Award, their most prestigious accolade. Other notable recipients include Walter Cronkite, Stephen Covey, Muhammad Yunus, and Zig Ziglar. Whether you're an aspiring speaker or looking to elevate your existing skills, Toastmasters is worth investigating.

For those interested in a professional speaking career, the National Speakers Association (NSA) is another organization to consider. Unlike Toastmasters, which focuses on skill-building for all levels, NSA is tailored to professional speakers who want to grow their careers in keynote speaking, training, and consulting. Members gain access to industry insights, networking opportunities, mentorship, and business-development resources. NSA also hosts events like the annual Influence Conference, where top speakers share strategies for branding, marketing, and audience engagement. Many well-known speakers, authors, and business consultants have built their careers through NSA connections and training. If you are looking to turn public speaking into a business or expand your reach as an authority, NSA provides an association that can support your ambitions. Learn more at www.toastmasters.org and nsaspeaker.org.

change to their businesses. I did my best to respond, drawing on data and examples, though it felt like I was barely keeping up. By the end, I managed to get through it and even changed a few minds. That experience, however, opened doors for me. After many similar presentations, I got much better. As I mentioned, I eventually became known as the "cheap Al Gore" on the speaking circuit—someone who could deliver "inconvenient truths" to business audiences for less than the six figures a former Vice President and Academy Award winner gets.

One of the best ways to take advantage of speaking opportunities is to collaborate with your school's public-relations, media, and marketing teams. These units often receive requests from community groups looking to have a professor speak to their members. These PR offices want to raise the profile of the school in the community. By proactively approaching these teams and offering to speak to community groups, you gain multiple benefits. First, you get the opportunity to speak in front of these groups and develop your skills and content. Second, your university office is effectively acting as your agent, looking for and booking speaking opportunities for you. And third, you are seen by the university administration as someone going beyond their duties and helping raise the school's community profile.

In one of my early faculty positions, shortly after I joined the school, I was asked to give a talk to a local business group. It was part of my service to the school, so I was happy to contribute, though I was a bit nervous. The presentation went well, and soon I found the school's press team inviting me a couple of times a year. Eventually, these talks became a regular part of my university service. For me, it was better than committee work. I even received formal recognition from the university for my contributions. The press-relations team saw value in my growing visibility and were actually amplifying my public profile, arranging media opportunities that helped establish my reputation as a thought leader.

Whether through your school or directly, when pitching these organizations, offer to speak on topics that align the organization's interests with your expertise. Creating a speaker profile that details your speaking topics, any previous engagements, and testimonials you received makes it easier for organizations to find and consider you. Proactively reaching out to organizations with a well-crafted pitch that highlights how your talk can benefit their audiences can help you secure a spot on the circuit and jump-start your reputation as a speaker.

Because these speaking engagements are usually uncompensated (except for the chewy chicken), you need to optimize the event for your personal branding and exposure. Host organizations usually do not have the experience or inclination to promote speakers beyond the basic announcement to their members. You need to be proactive in your self-promotion. First, inquire if the host organization publishes a newsletter, and ask that your speech be highlighted, both before and after the event. Propose a Q&A-style interview with the newsletter editor, or provide your own Q&A, answering questions you think the audience might ask. Alternatively, you can provide an article by you that showcases your expertise, the solutions you offer, your reputation as a speaker, and the relevance of your insights. Including your photograph with your story can significantly boost your visibility.

To get the most out of your engagement, be sure to have takeaways from the event that can be used in the future. For instance, creating a recording of your speech will be helpful for reviewing your performance and making improvements to your content and delivery. You will also want the recording for future promotional purposes. Having quality footage of you speaking commandingly in front of an audience is especially valuable. If you can get footage of the audience laughing, it can illustrate that you are not just competent but also entertaining. Many organizations can either film or make an audio recording of your presentations. Ask in your initial conversations if they intend to do so. If the organization cannot facilitate a recording, then arrange to do it yourself or with the help of a friend. You will probably need to ask the meeting planner if this is acceptable, since extra food for your photographer may be involved.

Also ask for a letter of recommendation or endorsement. Don't expect the organization to offer such a letter spontaneously. You will need to suggest it. In requesting a letter, you have several options. One is simply letting the organization write the best letter it can, which may or may not be helpful. A better option is to guide the organization on the topics to cover in the

Speaker Endorsements

Don't count on a host organization to produce a good endorsement letter for you. Instead, provide them with a sample letter, perhaps from a previous speech, along with a list of topics you'd like them to cover.

These topic headings can include:

- Your professional approach to planning and coordination with the committee

- Your quality program content

- The audience's positive response to your presentations

- Your receptivity to questions and approachability after the event

- Their desire to have you back in the future

Letters like this are invaluable social proof for future pitches and engagements.

letter to ensure it highlights your strengths effectively. Providing a sample letter from another organization can help. Ideally, you will build a file of letters, recordings, articles, and interviews from organizations where you have presented that you can use as materials on your website and in future promotion.

For a new speaker, leveraging LinkedIn endorsements is another strategic way to build speaker credibility. Before an event, you can network online with the organization's leadership. After each speaking engagement, follow up with the organizers and attendees you connected with, inviting them to connect on LinkedIn if they haven't already. Once connected, kindly request endorsements or recommendations on LinkedIn, specifically asking them to highlight aspects of your talk that resonated, such as the clarity of your presentation, the novelty of your ideas, or your engagement with the audience. Be specific in your request, suggesting they mention the event and what made your talk impactful. These personalized endorsements serve as social proof of your speaking skills and thought leadership, making you visible to your broader network and potential event organizers. Actively share content related to your speaking topics on LinkedIn, including insights from your talks, reflections on industry trends, and relevant articles. Engage with comments and discussions to further establish your expertise. Over time, this blend of endorsements and active online content will bolster your credibility, making you a more attractive candidate for higher-profile speaking engagements and solidifying your status as an emerging thought leader in your field.

Authority in Print: Writing a Thought Leader Book

As you build out your own platform, you will logically consider writing a book. A book can be an important part of your trajectory. It can serve as a vehicle to articulate and disseminate your unique insights and frameworks to a broad audience. Moreover, a book allows for the exploration of more complex ideas with the nuance and detail that shorter works or articles cannot afford, offering readers a more immersive and enlightening experience.

A book is also a useful tool for opening doors to speaking engagements, consulting opportunities, and further research collaborations. Historically, a published book has been a near requirement for obtaining paid speaking opportunities at major conferences, workshops, and seminars. Media outlets also privilege book authors in their coverage. And a book can boost your online presence through reviews, discussions, social-media interactions, and the like. It is no wonder that a book has been the quintessential calling card for thought leaders.

As you move along your development trajectory, think how your content and frameworks will come together in book form. By pursuing value-added curation, you will have a library of examples and source material that can support your manuscript. Any case studies you have written and taught can be folded into the overall book narrative. And your solutions to breakthrough problems can provide the larger framework for your book chapters. Most of my books have evolved out of this type of process, and I have learned to extract maximum value out of each element as I build to the eventual book treatment of the framework. By having this larger picture in mind, you can also think strategically about how these different elements will come together on your development trajectory.

Remember, as an academic authority, writing a book is not just about sharing knowledge; it's about shaping the conversation in your field and influencing current and future generations of leaders. A well-crafted book can become a legacy of your work.

Other People's Platforms

After a period of developing your personal platform and dining on rubber chickens, it's time to move up-circuit. With your core personal platform, some signature content, and assets like videos of your speaking, testimonials, and so on, you are prepared to engage more directly with your audience. You don't need a lot of these artifacts; in fact, a single video or audio recording of you speaking and a single testimonial are enough to get going. With this, you're poised to move up-circuit and engage with the trade and professional associations where your target audience is already congregating. Having mastered the art of creating impactful material, delivering it effectively, and navigating media relations, you're ready to reap the benefits of your work by positioning yourself in more prestigious and rewarding venues.

Through your synthesis work, you should be familiar with the main associations in your industry. You will have researched them, visited their websites, and requested and studied their advertising-information packets. You will understand their editorial thrust and the demographics of their membership.

The TED Talk

For a business-school professor aspiring to become a thought leader, delivering a TED Talk can be a useful milestone. TED Talks have become a global platform known for spreading innovative ideas and inspiring change across various disciplines, including business, technology, and education. By securing a spot on one of these stages, you can potentially amplify your reach and influence, presenting your insights to a worldwide audience, both in person and through the extensive online viewership TED Talks enjoy.

A well-delivered TED Talk not only showcases your expertise and communication skills but can also position you as a forward-thinking leader capable of distilling complex concepts into engaging, accessible narratives. This opportunity can lead to further speaking engagements, collaborations, and media appearances, thereby expanding your professional network and impact. Additionally, a TED Talk can serve as a potent teaching tool, providing students and peers with a model of clarity and passion in communication. A TED Talk offers a unique platform to inspire action, influence business practices, and contribute to shaping the future of their field.

Learn more about national and regional TED Talks at www.ted.com/talks.

You will have identified the editors responsible for online content as well as their conferences and have some foundational understanding of how these industry associations and their communication vehicles operate.

Most associations have platforms for guest contributions, including articles, blogs, podcasts, and interviews. Review the association's publications to understand the type of content they publish, and identify any content gaps or underrepresented topics. Based on this analysis, develop an initial article to pitch to the editors. Alternatively, you can propose an ongoing article series that offers unique insights or fills identified gaps. Take care in crafting the proposal, including an introduction to your credentials, your connection and engagement with the community, the series concept, potential article topics, and the expected outcomes for the audience. Your pitch should also include or point people back to the authority artifacts you have collected, like your endorsements, videos, articles, and other content. Use the editorial contacts within the association you have identified, and submit the proposal through the channels listed on the website or in a professional email.

If you have a strong proposal, associations are usually interested. They often have limited staff and resources, so they usually are looking to source additional content from outside the organization. Academics with a public profile outside academia are very attractive to these groups. Be prepared, however, for negotiation or feedback, and remain ready to adjust the proposal based on the association's needs. Once the concept is accepted, establishing a working relationship involves clarifying terms, such as copyright and author credits, and developing an editorial calendar for the series. Maintaining consistent quality and engaging with feedback from the association and its audience are essential for the success of the series and the ongoing relationship.

I have proposed and had multiple content series accepted by industry associations, such as Sustainable Brands, Energy & Environment Alliance, and GreenBiz. My multiple Sustainable Brands series, for example, have focused on the circular economy and sustainability strategy, both of which allowed me to raise my profile within these organizations. Through these publications, I connected with key figures in the sustainability community, leading to invitations for speaking engagements, panels, and collaborative offers. These series not only helped position me as a trusted voice in the field but also opened doors to industry opportunities. These can be compensated speaking engagements, something that will be discussed more in the next section. But you will want to use your speech in a similar way to what we discussed in the Rubber Chicken Circuit. By working closely with the professional association's team, you can maximize the meeting for the needs of both you and the organization.

ACADEMIC AUTHORITY

Again, you'll find that many organizations do not understand public relations and publicity. As with the Rubber Chicken Circuit, you can promote in advance of your presentation by suggesting an article about you. Writing an article from your unique perspective can foster a connection with your audience, allowing them to familiarize themselves with your ideas before the event and refer back afterwards. You should also inquire if the association sends out a media release to news outlets, including television, radio, newspapers, and magazines. If so, offer to contribute to the release by recommending compelling story angles about your work. You can also ask to have your remarks or a significant excerpt from your presentation featured in print after the event. However, it falls upon you to suggest this and work with the organization to find the right outlets for your work. Establishing yourself as a go-to thought leader in the community requires a proactive approach, and you should actively engage in shaping how you are presented to your intended audience, leveraging the opportunities to enhance your visibility and impact.

Some academic authorities I know build their entire authority career in service to a specific association. The previously mentioned Joe Cavinato, became an academic authority in supply-chain management and is a testament to strategic collaboration with an association. Early in his career, Cavinato recognized the importance of bridging the gap between academic research and industry practice in the supply-chain sector, leading him to work closely with the Institute of Supply Management (ISM). He contributed research, insights, and frameworks that addressed the challenges faced by supply-chain professionals. His active involvement in ISM's conferences, workshops, and publications not only disseminated his innovative ideas to a broader audience but also established him as a go-to expert in the field. By leveraging ISM's platform, Cavinato's contributions led the ISM to fund an endowed chair at his university, for which Cavinato was the founding professor. I learned from Joe, who graciously shared his experience with me, and, as a result, I was also able to become the founding chair holder of an endowed professorship that emerged out of engagement with a global business organization. Joe's work with ISM exemplifies how academics can advance their authority by aligning their research with the needs of a professional community they aim to serve, thereby making a lasting contribution to their field.

High Impact Practitioner Outlets

Building a robust platform and honing your skills as an authority are critical steps toward making significant contributions to high-impact practitioner outlets. This is the top of the circuit with journals like *Harvard Business Review*, *MIT Sloan Management Review*, and other outlets, such as *Forbes* or *Fast Company*. *HBR* and *SMR* are part of the *Financial Times* 50 list, a benchmark for business-school rankings. These outlets not only elevate your status as a thought leader but also contribute to the prestige and visibility of your institution.

A useful initial step in this journey is to aim for contributions to journals like the *California Management Review* or newer platforms like the *Management Business Review*. These journals serve as bridges between the academic and practitioner worlds, presenting rigorous research in a format that is accessible and applicable to practicing managers. While they maintain the scholarly standards through a peer-review process, their primary audience consists of business leaders and managers looking for cutting-edge insights and practical applications of research findings. This dual focus on academic rigor and practitioner relevance makes these journals excellent venues for academics seeking to expand their influence beyond the ivory tower and into the heart of industry practice.

Publishing in journals like *CMR* and *MBR* can be strategic for several reasons. First, it allows you to test and refine your ability to communicate complex ideas in a manner that resonates with business practitioners. Second, these contributions can significantly enhance your portfolio, demonstrating your capability to produce work that is both academically sound and practically relevant. Such a track record is often a prerequisite for consideration by the more-selective practitioner outlets. Lastly, engaging with the audience of these bridging journals helps to build a following among practicing managers, which can increase the impact and application of your research in real-world settings.

Beyond *CMR* and *MBR*, approaching high-impact journals such as *HBR* or *MIT SMR* necessitates a deliberate and strategic buildup of your professional profile. These outlets are inundated with submissions from around the world, making competition for publication fierce. The editors are seeking contributions that not only align with their editorial standards but also bring fresh insights and valuable content to their discerning readership. Editors of these journals do not have the time to nurture new talent, so you'll need to present upfront evidence of your abilities and reputation. Moving up-circuit provides you with numerous artifacts and publications that establish you as an authority, making you a better candidate for publication in these prestigious journals. Incrementally building your authority through speaking engagements, participation in industry panels, and contributing to well-regarded academic and practitioner outlets can significantly bolster your profile. By the time you're ready to pitch to outlets like *HBR* or *MIT SMR*, you should have a portfolio that showcases your ability.

Crafting an article pitch to prestigious outlets requires preparation. Begin by thoroughly researching both the type of content that the outlet typically publishes and its readership. You should read articles from the journal and deconstruct the style, voice, structure, topics, and journal sections. You can identify articles that resonate with you and that can serve as models for your piece. You should also check the editorial statements to get a sense of the journal's advertising demographics and statistics. You can also find the editors and follow them on LinkedIn or Twitter, something that can give you a better understanding of the editorial thrust and the different players in the journal.

This groundwork will help you tailor your pitch to align with their themes and the practical value they prioritize. Your pitch should start with a compelling hook or question that addresses a pressing issue or gap in the business world, demonstrating immediacy and relevance. Follow this with a brief overview of your unique insights or findings, emphasizing how they offer a new perspective or solution to the identified problem. Be sure to articulate the practical implications of your work, showing how it can be applied in real-world scenarios to drive improvement or innovation.

Additionally, outline the structure of your proposed article, including key arguments, evidence, and conclusions, to give editors a clear sense of its flow and content. Highlight your qualifications and previous publications to establish credibility and authority on the subject matter. It's also beneficial to acknowledge any previous articles or themes covered by the publication that relate to your pitch, showing how your work builds upon or diverges from existing discourse. It's critical to show that your article is a fresh take and not a reiteration or restatement of previous works. Your pitch should be concise, persuasive, and meticulously proofread, ensuring it communicates the value and uniqueness of your contribution effectively. Finally, be prepared to provide additional information or a more-detailed proposal if the editor expresses interest, demonstrating your commitment and readiness to engage with the publication process.

Once you have the interest of an editor, be patient and cooperative. They want to craft the best article possible and will work to improve on your initial draft. While you should push back if they are making factually incorrect suggestions, be open to their ideas and experience with what their readership expects.

By successfully publishing in these outlets, numerous new doors are likely to open to you. My ongoing *HBR* and *SMR* opportunities have arisen because I am a known quantity and have even been referred to as "part of the family." The imprimatur of these journals is also powerful for cultivating speaking engagements, corporate trainings, and more. I have traveled as a speaker and panelist for numerous *HBR* events in places like Miami, New York, and Doha, all of which were well compensated in addition to being high profile. For any aspiring academic authority, publishing in these outlets can be transformative. That said, I know of many successful authorities who have never been in these journals, finding instead outlets suited to their unique area of expertise. Do not feel obligated to pursue these opportunities to succeed as an authority.

This topic requires more space than available. For additional information on how to write an HBR-style article, see our video at www.globalleadershipacademy.com/HBR.

Setting the Stage for Compensated Opportunities

As you build a following through this value-driven communication, you position yourself to move into higher-level engagements, including compensated opportunities. Establishing a solid track record of delivering insights through these channels will naturally lead to speaking invitations, collaborations, and media opportunities that amplify your profile.

Ultimately, this approach sets the stage for you to capture significant value—whether through paid speaking engagements, consulting work, or publications. In the next chapter, we will explore how to convert your efforts into more tangible and compensated opportunities, ensuring that your authority is not only recognized but also rewarded.

• • •

Part III

Beyond Authority: Capturing Value

CHAPTER 10

An Authority Enterprise Beyond the Ivory Tower

As an academic thought leader, your primary goal may be to shape managerial thinking, influence practice, and establish intellectual authority. This pursuit is an end in itself. Others, however, may seek to go a step further—leveraging their influence to enhance their financial security and well-being. As I mentioned, in my case, I initially pursued my practitioner work in response to the lack of content and frameworks in my field. Along the way, I found that the engagement with practitioners was stimulating and rewarding. I did not initially consider the potential material benefits that helping to solve the real-world problems of managers might confer.

I first discovered that what I was doing might be valuable when I was asked early on by my university's PR team to consider a request they had from an industry conference that was coming to town and was looking for a speaker. Like I had done before, I thought of this as university and community service and reached out to the event organizers. They were enthusiastic about my topic idea and invited me to speak at the conference. I thought that was the end of it when they said, "Unfortunately, we only have the budget to pay you $3,000 . . ." I mumbled something like, ". . . that will be fine" and then got off the phone. I had received a $500 honorarium before, but here someone was offering me $3,000 for 60 minutes of my time, and they were apologizing because it was such a paltry sum. That was my first introduction to what can be called the authority or expert industry.

Since that time, many other opportunities to receive compensation for my work have arisen without me actively pursuing it. And the experiences have been interesting.

For instance, it turns out that there is a secret cabin in the nose of a 747 airliner where you'll find four to six seats for passengers. A better word than seats might be "spaces" because these are individual islands to themselves. The cabin is manned by two dedicated flight attendants, making for an impressive attendant-to-passenger ratio. Like ex-ed faculty, these attendants gain access to the most elite passengers but only after working their way up to the cabin. They start in coach, moving to business class, and then to first class, until they finally make it to the very tip of the plane.

I know, because I once scored a seat—or space—in the nose of a 747.

As a lifelong coach passenger, finding myself in this elite travel class—a world reserved for CEOs and other ultra-wealthy individuals—was a bit surreal. Having spent my career traveling in cramped economy seats, this level of travel was a revelation. The spaciousness, the personalized service—it was an entirely new world.

I had been researching a major international holding company, studying their efforts to implement a comprehensive values framework across multiple companies in diverse business sectors. At one point, I was invited to their global headquarters, located halfway around the world, and they handled all my travel details. I was told I would be traveling business class, but when I got to the gate, the attendant told me I had been upgraded by the company.

While everyone else turned right on entering the plane, heading back to the main cabins, I was told to go left, passing through first class to the forward-most room. I was escorted to my seat and offered a pre-flight aperitif. Once I was seated, the attendant engaged me in some enchanting banter while serving an appetizer accompanied by a glass of Champagne. After takeoff, I was offered an elegant four-course meal with tailored wine flights chosen by the airline's sommelier. It was a long way from being tossed a bag of peanuts.

Dessert was a hot-fudge sundae with French vanilla ice cream crafted to my taste by the attendant. I capped off the meal with an aged cognac served in a snifter, warmed tableside with hot water.

Following dinner, I received a wrapped package containing pajamas. When I was ready, I could go to the wardrobe and change. In the meantime, the attendant would prepare my bed. When I returned, my seat was lying perfectly flat. A memory foam mattress had been placed atop, and Egyptian cotton sheets were laid out. As I slid into my bed, the attendant tucked me in for a good night's sleep. I arrived a dozen time zones away more refreshed than when I had left.

That experience ruined travel for me forever.

I share this not just because it was a fun experience, but because it highlights the kind of opportunities and access that becoming an academic authority can offer. And while the luxuries are nice, I still find the real value lies in the access—being part of conversations that influence key decisions and having the chance to make an impact beyond academia. Getting invited to the World Economic Forum in Davos, Switzerland, and other global confabs opens a world very different from the ivory tower. From events at the Beverly Hills hotel with A-list celebrities to meetings in China with world leaders, I've found that academic authorities are given access to the world of consequential decisions where our expertise can influence events.

Of course, there are also risks and pitfalls. It's easy to be dazzled by the perks. With those perks comes the responsibility to maintain your academic integrity. Navigating corporate relationships requires a careful balance—one where you can't let the allure of corporate luxuries compromise your ability to provide honest, unbiased insights. An academic authority must be careful to protect their professional integrity. They must remain vigilant and ensure their ability to call things as they are is never challenged. You are not a hired gun, like a corporate consultant or accountant. You are an academic authority.

But while the business-class lifestyle and entrée into the halls of power is gratifying, for me and the other authorities I interviewed, there is a far greater reward—a higher purpose to our work. When our ideas are put into practice and help businesses solve real-world problems, that's when we know we're doing something truly meaningful. Beyond the perks, it's about shaping the future of business and making a real difference. During my interviews, more than one authority quoted Steve Jobs to me: "We are here to put a dent in the universe."

Many of us have insights that could put a dent in the universe, but traditional academic channels often limit our reach. Becoming a thought leader allows you to extend your influence beyond the ivory tower, giving you the platform to share your knowledge with those who need it most.

An Authority Enterprise

The expert or authority industry is a well-developed ecosystem that supports big-name thought leaders in building and monetizing their expertise through speaking, publishing, and consulting. At the center of this industry, you find meeting planners organizing corporate events as well as speaker bureaus like the Washington Speakers Bureau (WSB) and Gotham Artists acting as agents to secure high-profile speaking engagements. On the publishing side, you find book agents helping experts land deals with major publishers. There are also media coaches and PR firms that book interviews, podcasts, and thought-leadership columns in top outlets. At these levels, you find people like Wharton's Adam Grant, with his bestselling books, popular TED podcast, and contributions to *Harvard Business Review* and *The New York Times*. You also find world leaders like former President Barack Obama, with his books and high-profile keynote addresses. Grant and Obama exemplify the interconnected industry that helps experts not only establish their authority but also turn their knowledge into a sustainable business and global influence.

Some of you here may aspire to reach these heights, and some of you may succeed. But you do not have to be a celebrity at the level of Obama to be materially rewarded for your authority work. Modern digital technologies have lowered barriers, making it easier than ever for academics and thought leaders to reach their audience directly and offer their expertise. Online courses, webinars, and membership communities enable you to package and offer your knowledge to a global audience. Additionally, tools like Zoom allow for virtual consulting and Substack for subscription-based content, providing new revenue opportunities that were unimaginable just a few years ago. Whether through paid newsletters, online workshops, or self-published books, academic authorities can now create value and capture their share of it—on their own terms.

The following chapter lays out the basic ways an authority can package and offer their expertise for compensation. As mentioned, this is an optional chapter. Some of you will be satisfied making a contribution to practice through your work. Others may be interested in enhancing your financial security and well-being by expanding the potential income streams available to you. And still others may just be curious about this emerging business sector. Whatever your interest, the following chapter intends to give you an overview of the interesting world of the authority industry.

•••

CHAPTER 11

Capturing Your Share of Your Created Value

Up to this point, we've explored the steps necessary to establish yourself as an academic authority within a practitioner community. Now, we shift our focus toward capturing financial value from your authority platform. You should be fairly compensated for the value you're creating for your audience. In this chapter, we will explore seven key ways to package your expertise and how each could be structured to potentially double your faculty salary as you amplify your impact as an academic authority. To do so, you need to package your expertise and your solution frameworks and make them available to your audience.

As discussed, compensation can be a touchy subject with academics, and there are often strong, deeply rooted opinions about compensating academics for practitioner work. Some academic authorities I've interviewed refuse to mention, or even acknowledge, the fact that one can be compensated for their expertise. This hesitation has partly to do with the nature of scientific discovery. Most academics embrace an open-source ethos, underpinning contributions to scientific understanding. Many value the pursuit of knowledge for its own sake and openly share their professional insights with their peers to advance collective understanding. The idea that knowledge should be freely disseminated without expectation of financial gain can be at odds with the idea of monetizing expertise. Moreover, academia privileges peer recognition and contributions to one's field over financial rewards, leading to an aversion to expressing expertise in monetary terms. It's tricky, therefore, to balance one's contribution to the advancement of knowledge with fair compensation for value created by specialized expertise.

Yet, as discussed in earlier chapters, there is a good argument for being more open about this aspect of academic thought leadership. Acknowledging the value of your academic expertise not only recognizes the tangible impact of your work but also highlights the professional responsibilities of business schools to contribute to practice. When academics generate value for managers, they deliver improvements in organizational practice, strategy, and outcomes. Compensation in this light becomes a natural consequence of the value provided. Being open about compensation can, therefore, encourage a more-balanced view of academia's role in society. Generating and sharing knowledge, while inherently valuable, also warrants fair remuneration when it drives tangible benefits outside the boundaries of academic discourse.

Beyond professional considerations, there's also a practical aspect to being compensated, an aspect that often goes unrecognized: *Your audience's perception of authority is significantly influenced by the relative value of those solutions.* Simply put, if you want to be perceived as an authority, you should have solutions for sale.

While publications and citations can establish your expertise among academics, there's a transformative moment in your practitioner audience's perception when you transition from merely sharing knowledge to providing actionable solutions with tangible value. It signals to your audience that your insights are not only useful but also valuable in solving real-world problems. The act of selling a solution, whether it's a book, a consulting service, or an online course, serves as a powerful endorsement of your authority. It implicitly communicates that your expertise is not only recognized but also sought after, reinforcing your status as a thought leader who goes beyond theory to offer practical, impactful guidance.

This dynamic underscores a key lesson from earlier chapters: Authority is not just creating knowledge but also packaging and positioning it in a way that meets the needs and expectations of your audience. Fortunately, as an academic authority, there are a handful of primary ways you can package and offer your solutions. We will cover each of these approaches in this chapter. Using any one of them could provide a handsome additional revenue stream for you, but most authorities build out a mix of different offers to meet the needs of different market segments.

For example, you might sell books and also deliver keynote speeches. Or perhaps you'll offer an online course alongside running a seminar, while also engaging in coaching. We will delve into book publishing, speaking engagements, online courses, and in-person seminars, subscription programs, consulting, and developing a coaching program. The good news is that these avenues don't require specialized tools or permissions to get started. Everything you need is readily available to you today.

By building a reputation beyond your faculty position and establishing a secondary income stream, you'll build a more-secure financial future. Earning income as an academic authority can help achieve important life goals. My extramural work has helped me finance top-tier education for my children, fund my retirement accounts, and spend valuable time with my aging parents, among other family benefits. But beyond the material benefits, I find it deeply gratifying to be acknowledged by people who have been impacted by my work.

For myself and the many authorities I've had the privilege of interviewing, financial gain is not the driving force. The true motivation lies in the exhilaration of uncovering new insights and the satisfaction of contributing meaningful advancements to practice. This intrinsic motivation stems from a desire to see our work contribute to solving real-world problems, to witness the tangible impact of our work on individuals and society at large—in essence, to leave a lasting legacy. Consequently, compensation is not the goal but a natural byproduct of a commitment to generating and sharing substantial value. In this light, money is a metric to measure the effectiveness and worth of our contributions rather than the primary objective of our authority journeys.

ACADEMIC AUTHORITY

Valuing Your Expertise

Since we are going to be open about compensation, you might ask: *How much money can an authority figure actually make?* Frankly, the sky's the limit. Take, for instance, celebrity academic authorities, like Harvard Business School's Michael Porter, who commands $150,000 for a single speech. His late colleague Clayton Christensen received around $100,000 per speech. Of course, you and I are not Michael Porter or Clayton Christensen, so it may be hard to imagine this level of compensation. In fact, a number of academics I have spoken with have openly wondered why anyone would pay them at all for their expertise. When we discuss their past experiences, I find that most never even receive an honorarium for speeches. For some reason, they vastly underestimate the value of their know-how.

Part of their skepticism comes from the relative cost of creating and delivering solutions. With today's technology and tools, creating programs and products can be easy and low cost. For example, say you wanted to create an audio program like "negotiating salaries" or "condominium valuation" or some other topic that addresses your audience's concerns. All you would need is your computer, a good quality microphone, and audio-recording software, like GarageBand, which comes installed for free on every Apple device. That's it. After you record your program, you can post your audio files on a website, make them available for download, and begin offering your solution to your audience. The cost of creating your solution is basically your time invested. The cost of delivering it is a rounding error, thanks to digital distribution. Nevertheless, a typical audio course like this can range in price from $30 to $300, maybe more. Given this, I have heard academics wonder why anyone would pay such a high price for such a cheap-to-produce product?

My best answer comes from an old story my mechanic used to tell me before he handed me his repair bill. I had a bad habit of buying older British roadsters, and these cars had their own bad habits of breaking down frequently. This led to repeated meetings with my mechanic and arguments about the costs of repairs. To soften me up for the bill, the mechanic would

Capturing Your Share of Your Created Value

tell me the story of a boilermaker who was hired to repair a faulty steamship engine boiler.

The ship's captain, the story goes, described the problem to the boilermaker, who asked a handful of follow-up questions. He then went into the ship's massive boiler room and began inspecting the twisting labyrinth of pipes. After a few minutes of listening to the growls and hiss of escaping steam, he felt some pipes with his hands. He then reached into his overalls, took out a small hammer, and gave a single quick tap on a bright red valve. Immediately the entire system shuddered, and then began working perfectly. The ship's captain was overjoyed, and the boilermaker went home.

A week later, the steamship captain received a bill from the boilermaker for $1,000. He was outraged! How could the boilermaker demand so much money? He had only been in the engine room for a few minutes! And then all he did was tap a valve with his little hammer. How could this possibly merit a bill of $1,000? In a huff, the captain ordered the boilermaker to send him an itemized bill.

So, the boilermaker sent the following bill:

- Tapping the valve: $.50
- Knowing where to tap: $999.50
- TOTAL: $1,000.00

Academic authorities, like the boilermaker, have accumulated substantial specialized expertise. If you can tell an executive where to tap, you have something of massive value. The value of your solution has little to do with the cost of creating the product or packaging it. Your specialized knowledge is not a commodity. You may not imagine that someone would pay you $1,000 for an online training program or $2,500 to attend your three-day seminar, but if you know where to tap, you can save people time and money and accelerate their success. Do not underestimate the value of your knowledge and your solutions. As an academic authority, you may be selling more than just knowledge—you're offering a shortcut to success, which should be priced appropriately.

ACADEMIC AUTHORITY

Your Frameworks, Your Assets

As discussed in previous chapters, your solution frameworks are not just theoretical constructs; they are assets. An "asset" is defined as a resource with economic value that can be used to generate future revenue streams. Assets can be tangible, like real estate, equipment, and inventory, or intangible, such as patents, trademarks, copyrights, and goodwill. The key characteristic is the asset's potential to create a future stream of income, thereby contributing to the wealth and financial security of the holder. Proper management and strategic utilization of these assets are crucial for maximizing their potential return. As such, it's crucial to think of these frameworks as intellectual property (IP), and you should safeguard the integrity and ownership of this IP. Maintaining control of your solution content ensures that you, as the creator, dictate how and where your work is used, shared, and monetized. This approach not only protects your intellectual contributions, but it also maximizes their impact and value with the broader practitioner community.

For an example of how a solution framework can form the foundational asset of an authority enterprise, consider the late Dr. Stephen R. Covey, author of *The 7 Habits of Highly Effective People*. Covey started his career as a professor at Brigham Young University's Marriott School of Management, where he chaired the organizational behavior department. In 1984, Covey established the Covey Leadership Center and began developing the framework that would become the 7 Habits. After publication of the book, the Covey Center merged with Franklin Quest, a company known for its time-management workshops and the Franklin Planner, a planning system popular with managers.

The new company, FranklinCovey Co., began building a business around Covey's intellectual property. The 7 Habits became a teachable, trainable, and scalable framework. Covey's book sold more than 25 million copies worldwide, was translated into 40 languages, and is considered a seminal text in the self-help and personal-productivity genres. The company expanded the framework's reach beyond the book by developing a comprehensive suite of training programs that operationalized the 7-Habits principles for different markets, offering workshops and seminars to organizations and individuals wanting to implement the habits in their work and lives.

Multiple Revenue Streams from a Single Framework Asset

Stephen Covey's Seven Habits illustrates the financial potential of managing solution frameworks as assets. The personal-development and corporate-training programs built around Covey's framework have different pricing tiers to accommodate market segments:

For *individuals* attending open-enrollment workshops or online courses, prices can range from a few hundred to several thousand dollars, depending on the depth and duration of the program. For example, the FranklinCovey Academy offers an eight-module online course for five hundred and fifty dollars. They also offer live in-person courses that vary in price.

On the other hand, *organizations*, including corporations, nonprofits, and governments, can bring FranklinCovey-certified trainers into their establishments to deliver programs to their employees. Pricing here is tailored to the size of the group, the level of customization required, and the logistical costs associated with on-site training. These engagements can range from tens of thousands to more than a hundred thousand dollars for extensive, company-wide programs.

Because Covey and the company designed the framework to be teachable and scalable, they can train other people to deliver the material through *Trainer Certification*. For professionals looking to become certified trainers of the 7 Habits framework, the process involves extensive training, assessment, and ongoing support. The investment for certification can be several thousand dollars, and, after the initial certification, there are also renewal fees to maintain status as a FranklinCovey Certified Trainer. These fees can vary but are usually paid annually as an ongoing revenue stream.

Besides the direct cost of the program, implementation requires *supplementary materials*, such as texts, workbooks, and online resources, which are made available for separate purchase. Additionally, access to digital learning platforms or subscription-based content can add ongoing costs for participants or organizations wishing to maintain access to these resources.

ACADEMIC AUTHORITY

The framework and training can also be licensed and offered by third-party organizations. For example, Cornell University has delivered a three-day version of the program called "The 7 Habits of Highly Effective People 4.0." The American Management Association (AMA), a global professional organization with a number of professional-development programs, delivers a version of the "7 Habits of Highly Effective People" course ranging in price from $2,395 for members to $2,695 for non-members. It offers the course in different global locations several times per month.

Beyond the core offerings, the framework has inspired several programs targeted at different audiences and contexts. For example, the company offers a version called "7 Habits of Highly Effective Teens" to help young people build self-confidence and interpersonal skills. It is usually taught in community-based settings, such as after-school programs or faith-based organizations. And, of course, to facilitate scaling of the programs, FranklinCovey provides the "7 Habits for Teens" training program to prepare and certify educators, administrators, and parents as trainers.

All of these diverse offerings emerged from a single solution framework created by an academic authority. With the support of this framework, Covey and his team were able to build a company with 1,000 employees and an annual revenue of more than $200 million per year.

With his frameworks, Covey not only solidified his status as a thought leader but also demonstrated the potential of academic ideas to generate economic value and lasting impact. Through his work, Covey extended his influence beyond publishing to include corporate training and organizational consulting.

Covey, of course, did not stop with the 7 Habits. He subsequently authored several other influential books, including *First Things First*, *Principle-Centered Leadership*, *The 8th Habit: From Effectiveness to Greatness*, and *The Leader in Me*. Covey's contributions have been recognized with numerous awards, including the International Entrepreneur of the Year Award, the National Entrepreneur of the Year Lifetime Achievement Award for Entrepreneurial Leadership, and the McFeely Award from the International Management Council for significant contributions to management and leadership.

The success of Covey's framework can be attributed to its applicability and the actionable steps, underscoring the importance of envisioning how solution frameworks as assets can be packaged, taught, and scaled in ways that extend their reach and relevance.

Packaging Your Frameworks

As stated, to be seen as an authority, having branded offerings provides tangible proof of your expertise and the value of your authority. Fortunately, there are only a handful of core ways to package your frameworks and content. The process of packaging your solutions can be conceptualized on a "Value-Added Spectrum" that transitions from free to fee. This spectrum begins with freely available content designed to add value to your audience without immediate financial return, setting the foundation for your authority. We've discussed the free end of the spectrum in the previous chapters.

Value-Added Spectrum: from Free to Fee

As you progress along the spectrum, the value—and, consequently, the price—of your offerings increases. Several factors contribute to this escalation in value. First, the content becomes more comprehensive, offering deeper insights and step-by-step solutions. Equally critical is the increasing level of access the audience gets to you, the academic authority. Starting with articles and progressing through books, speeches, seminars, and ultimately to consulting, each step further along the spectrum not only offers more tailored content but also intensifies the interaction between you and your audience. By enhancing the personalized nature of the experience, you increase the value for the audience. This journey from free content to high-value, fee-based engagements encapsulates the essence of transforming your authority into a sustainable and rewarding enterprise.

The subsequent sections will discuss each of these value-adding formats. Again, most authorities will deliver some mix of the different formats depending on the needs of their audience and their personal preferences.

A Road Map to Doubling Your Faculty Salary

As we've said, certain celebrity academic authorities command tens of thousands of dollars for a single keynote address. This demonstrates the upper echelon of potential earnings, but let's consider a more relatable benchmark for most of us—the average professor's salary. What would it take to double your salary as an academic authority?

According to the Association to Advance Collegiate Schools of Business (AACSB), at the entry-level, assistant professors in business schools typically earn $80,000 to $120,000 per year, depending on the institution and field of study, while full professors can earn upwards of $200,000 per year. The average tenured associate professor earns $100,000 to $120,000. So, for illustration purposes we can ask what it would take to generate an additional $100,000 a year by offering your packaged solution frameworks. We will explore how each of the potential offerings could be used to generate an additional $100,000 a year. Generating this level of income is obviously not guaranteed, yet many experts with fewer credentials than you earn significantly more than this.

Capturing Your Share of Your Created Value

Authorship

As discussed, one of the most popular and traditional ways to establish yourself as a thought leader is by publishing a book. It's no coincidence that the root word of "authority" is "author." Historically, authorities have depended upon traditional publishing houses to get their names in print. However, with the tools and technologies available today, nearly anyone can self-publish a book. Both avenues offer benefits and limitations.

Traditional publishing involves signing a contract with an established publishing house to produce, distribute, and market your book. This path offers some advantages, including professional editing, design, and some marketing services, along with potential distribution to bookstores. Authorities pursuing this route benefit from the credibility and prestige associated with well-known publishers. However, the process of securing a traditional publishing deal can be competitive, with long timelines from manuscript submission to publication. Additionally, royalty rates offered by traditional publishers are generally lower, reflecting the services provided by the publisher.

Royalties are payments that authors receive as compensation for the sale of their book, essentially a percentage of the revenue generated from each book sold. The rate at which royalties are paid can vary significantly depending on the publishing agreement, the format of the book (e.g., hardcover, paperback, eBook), and the sales channels through which the book is sold.

In a traditional-publishing arrangement, royalty rates for printed books typically range from 10% to 15% of the book's list price, depending on the number of copies sold. For eBooks, the rates can be higher, often between 25% and 50% of the net sale price. These percentages can vary based on the publisher's policies and the negotiation between the author and the publisher. For example, an author might receive a 10% royalty on the first 5,000 copies, increasing to 12.5% for the next 10,000 copies, and 15% for all subsequent sales.

To achieve $100,000 in book royalty payments, we have to look into the mechanics of how a traditional-publishing agreement might reach this target. Assuming a hardcover book carries a retail price of $25, and the author's contract stipulates a 10% royalty on the list price, each sale would net the author $2.50. To amass $100,000 from hardcover sales, you would need to sell 40,000 copies—a substantial milestone given that the average business book sells between 2,000 to 3,000 copies in its lifetime. While some business books by celebrity authors that capture the zeitgeist of the moment can sell tens of thousands of copies, books by less-known authors or with niche topics might sell fewer than 1,000 copies.

This simplified analysis doesn't account for potential variations in royalty rates, but it illustrates the scale of sales required to achieve significant royalty payments. It also illuminates a saying among many established thought leaders: "There are lots of best-selling authors who are broke." Many first-time authors imagine that, once their book is published, their future success is secured and that money and offers will come pouring in. However, unless you are J. K. Rowling, a traditional publishing deal is unlikely to set you up for retirement. While a book published by a prestigious publishing house can provide substantial credibility for you, your royalty expectations should be modest.

An alternative to traditional publishing is self-publishing. While self-publishing platforms often offer higher royalty rates, the tradeoff is that the author assumes more of the responsibility for the editing, design, and marketing of the book. However, in reality, the responsibility for marketing your book will fall almost entirely on you whether you self-publish or work with a traditional publisher. Gone are the days when your publisher organized a nationwide book tour for you, with appearances on the *Today Show* and Oprah. In fact, one of the things a publishing house will want to know before they offer you a contract is how big of a "platform" you have. Your platform is essentially the strategic amalgamation of various channels, content, and frameworks that you have created in the early stages of your development trajectory. The publisher wants you to have a robust digital presence through websites, blogs, and social-media profiles that ideally have thousands of followers that make a ready market for your book.

You may ask yourself, if I have to do all of the marketing of my book anyway, do I only want to receive a 10% royalty? Alternative platforms like Amazon's Kindle Direct Publishing (KDP) can offer up to 70% of an eBook's sale price as royalties in certain markets. While there are times when traditional publishing

Self-Publishing Tasks

When self-publishing, authors take on tasks traditionally handled by publishing houses. Here's a breakdown of some of the tasks that a traditionally published author would typically delegate to a publisher, but that a self-publishing author would need to manage on their own:

1. **Editing and proofreading**: Beyond just writing the manuscript, self-published authors need to ensure their work is free of grammatical errors, typos, and inconsistencies. This often involves hiring professional editors or proofreaders to refine the manuscript.

2. **Design and formatting**: The visual appeal of a book, including its cover design and interior layout, plays a crucial role in attracting readers. Self-publishers must either design and format their books themselves or outsource these tasks to professionals.

3. **ISBN acquisition and copyright registration**: Obtaining an ISBN (International Standard Book Number) and registering copyright are essential steps in the publishing process that ensure a book is recognized and protected as a unique publication.

4. **Distribution and sales channels**: Traditional publishers have established relationships with distributors and retailers, both online and in brick-and-mortar stores, which they use to sell and distribute books. Self-publishing authors must research and select distribution platforms, such as Amazon's Kindle Direct Publishing or IngramSpark, and actively manage their presence on these platforms.

5. **Marketing and promotion**: While authors are increasingly expected to participate in marketing activities regardless of their publishing route, self-published authors bear full responsibility for promoting their books.

> 6. **Legal and financial management**: Self-published authors are responsible for understanding the legalities of publishing, including copyright law and contracts, if they hire freelance professionals.
>
> Navigating the process requires authors to wear many hats, from creative director to marketing strategist to business manager. While self-publishing offers greater creative control and the potential for higher royalties, it also demands additional personal investment.

makes the most sense, for many academic authorities that have established relationships with associations and an audience, self-publishing can be more lucrative.

Another key consideration: In traditional publishing, you sign over the copyright to your content to your publisher. Do you want to turn over control of your most valuable asset to someone else?

The process of self-publishing has become surprisingly straightforward in the digital age, making it an accessible option for many. While some people manage the entire publishing process themselves—from writing and copyediting to formatting and cover design—others opt to leverage the talents of low-cost freelance gig workers for certain tasks. In my experience, I enlisted the help of an art major from my university to craft the cover and graphics for a book and hired a copy editor to ensure the text was polished and error-free. Once your book is ready, the transition to distribution is seamless, especially with platforms like Amazon Books simplifying the process. Uploading your digital file to Amazon allows you to offer your book in various formats, including hardcover, paperback, and Kindle versions, directly from their platform. This ease of self-publishing opens up significant opportunities for authorities.

In the realm of self-publishing, platforms like Amazon can offer authors royalty rates of approximately 35%, significantly higher than the traditional publishing industry's standard of around 10%. This increase in royalty rates presents a notable opportunity for authors to increase the income from their work. For instance, if you wanted to generate $100,000 in royalties at a net income of $5.74 per book, you would need to sell approximately 17,422 copies of your book. That is still a lot of books, but it is less than half the number needed if you were to go the traditional-publisher route.

Another alternative with self-publishing is to skirt the Amazon-type distributors altogether and leverage direct digital distribution. Through your website, you can offer a digital version of your book directly to your audience. In this situation you can basically retain 100% of the sales revenue. By self-distributing a digital version of your book, you eliminate intermediary fees, thereby maximizing earnings. Moreover, the pricing of your book can be strategically set to reflect its value. Especially for technical or specialized content, you can command higher prices. Academics understand this dynamic because of textbook pricing. It is not uncommon for textbooks for undergraduate courses to cost $80 to $150, with some specialized or highly technical textbooks costing upwards of $200.

Let's consider a scenario where you self-publish a comprehensive guide for professionals in your field. You decide to sell a digital version of the book directly to your audience through your website at a price at $49.95. To generate an additional $100,000 in annual revenue, you need to sell approximately 2,000 copies a year. That is a much more reasonable number than either the traditional publisher or Amazon route offers. If you could sell around 170 copies each month, you could effectively double the average professor's salary every year. And, of course, if you are able to raise the value and price further, the number of needed sales declines.

By self-publishing and using near-zero-cost digital distribution, you can capture nearly 100% of potential revenue from your book. You also maintain full ownership and control over your content. As we will see, this content can be packaged in many formats and offered to your audience.

ACADEMIC AUTHORITY

Speaking and Webinars

Another way you can package your content for audience delivery is public speaking. If you followed the suggestions in the previous chapter, you will have had some initial speaking engagements and should have developed some stage skills and material. Over time, you will derive this material from your solution frameworks. In journeying from academic to speaker, you won't create a single speech, but rather a repertoire of presentations that are diverse both in content and format. Seasoned professional speakers often have a portfolio of two or three dozen programs, each targeting a different topic and audience. At this early stage, you will want to develop a core topic from which you can generate derivative presentations. Tailoring a program to different durations, from short speeches to multi-day workshops, gives you flexibility in presentation and audience engagement.

For example, when I developed my sustainability-strategy content, I was initially offering a standard 45–60 minute keynote, providing an overview of the frameworks. From here, I created a half-day workshop that incorporated audience participation and case discussions of the material. For executive-education offerings, this was expanded into full-day workshops that included exercises applying the frameworks to real-world problems. I ultimately created a full semester-long treatment of the materials that included my own textbook and cases that can be delivered in a variety of formats. This suite of offerings enabled me to meet the diverse needs of my audiences, providing tailored content while maintaining the integrity of my core sustainability-strategy frameworks.

With a single core program, you can begin targeting professional associations for speaking opportunities. As part of your initial authority-development trajectory, you will have been examining the agendas of the conventions within your field and identifying gaps or opportunities where a new program could offer value. Your approach should begin with a thoughtful proposal that demonstrates your understanding of the organization's needs and how your presentation can meet them. Discussing fees in your initial outreach depends on your status in the community and your established presence as a

Diversifying and Scaling Your Content Delivery

By starting with a core program, you can then branch out into varied formats. Doing so allows you to offer tailored content for virtually any scenario, using a consistent base of knowledge. Here are some typical content formats to offer your audience:

- standard 45–60 minute keynote

- 2–2.5 hour workshop incorporating some audience participation

- half-day workshop designed for more interactive engagement

- full-day workshop focusing on in-depth problem-solving and participant involvement

- two-day workshop encouraging participants to engage in written exercises

- five-day institute or seminar with extensive lectures, assignments, and other speakers

speaker. Regardless, the aim is to present yourself as a valuable asset to the organization, capable of delivering insightful, engaging content that meets the immediate needs and interests of its members.

After refining your core program into distinct formats, the next step is to develop related programs that resonate with your target market. By reusing and repurposing content across different formats and audiences, you maximize the value of your solution frameworks. Once an organization recognizes the value of your initial program, your goal is to be invited back with either updated content or entirely new presentations in the future. This strategy not only maintains your relevance but also strengthens your relationship with the organization, potentially leading to more speaking opportunities.

Fees for speaking engagements vary significantly. As an academic, even without having firmly established yourself as an authority, it's feasible to command around $2,000 per speech. This fee is quite attainable if you're knowledgeable, able to negotiate effectively, and can offer an engaging topic. By earning $2,000 per speech and conducting one talk a month you can accumulate $24,000 a year—not an insignificant sum. However, moving up to the higher end of the speaker-fee spectrum can quickly increase your earnings. Once you've solidified your reputation as a speaker, especially if you've honed your platform skills, fees can reach $8,000 per engagement, often times more. At this speaking fee, one speech per month would nearly double that $100,000 faculty salary.

Book authorship is another way to increase your speaking fees, illustrating how the different content formats can work together synergistically. Having a published book can position you into a higher echelon of speaking fees and open doors to speaking to corporate clients. Delivering speeches for $10,000 or even $20,000 for international engagements, is quite common among professional speakers with a published book. And there are usually opportunities to further enhance your engagement income beyond speaking fees. Often you can have the organization offer your book for sale to attendees and arrange a book-signing event after your presentation. Selling a few hundred additional books can substantially boost your event compensation.

For those less inclined toward traditional public speaking or travel, conducting webinars from the comfort of your home offers a viable alternative. The financial potential of these engagements depends on the quality and value of your content. The cost of a business-training webinar varies based on factors like the topic's complexity, the presenter's expertise, the duration of the webinar, and the level of interactivity involved. On average, prices can range from as low as $100 or less for basic, pre-recorded sessions, to upward of $500 or more for live, interactive webinars led by renowned experts. Some high-end or specialized business-training webinars, especially those offering certification or advanced training, can cost several thousand dollars. Additionally, many organizations and trainers offer tiered pricing based on the number of participants, with discounts for larger groups or corporate packages.

If you were able to create a training webinar and priced it at the low end of $99, offering it just once per month, you would need about 80 attendees to generate about $100,000 per year. Again, there are also opportunities to enhance your income by offering your book or other specialized materials with your program. However, increasing the complexity and completeness of your program quickly moves you out of the webinar and speaking space and into seminar and online-course formats.

Seminars and Online Courses

Some of the most valuable formats for academic authorities are seminars and online courses. The business-seminar industry began in the 1950s as an extension of university offerings on topics like accounting and efficiency in operations, reflecting the industrial era's emphasis on productivity and scientific management. Over time, these original programs evolved into the executive-education programs offered by many business schools today.

Outside of academia, there was a significant boom in business seminars during the 1970s and '80s, partly fueled by the self-help movement and a growing emphasis on leadership and soft skills as key components of business success. It was during this era that the high-profile motivational speaker and business guru started to dominate the scene, offering seminars that promised not only to impart knowledge but also to inspire and transform attendees.

The advent of the internet and digital technology further transformed the business-seminar industry in the late 20th and early 21st centuries with online webinars, virtual conferences, and e-learning platforms. This digital shift allowed for a broader range of topics, more interactive formats, and the ability to reach participants across different geographical locations, all at a lower cost than traditional in-person seminars. Today, the management-seminar business is a multifaceted industry that encompasses a wide array of formats, from conferences to online events, catering to a growing demand for lifelong learning and professional development. Increasingly, there is an emphasis on not just technical skills but also soft skills, adaptability, and resilience.

In-person seminars can be incredibly lucrative. However, they require substantial infrastructure to run them. To deliver an in-person seminar to a few hundred people, you would need to arrange for a suitable venue that can comfortably accommodate the audience size, equipped with seating, acoustics, and climate control. You would need reliable audio-visual equipment, including a sound system for clear audio delivery, microphones (both handheld and lapel for mobility), a projector and screen for presentations, and potentially a stage or platform for visibility. Behind the scenes, logistical support staff would be needed for registration, attendee management, and customer service to ensure a smooth operation. Furthermore, provisions for refreshments or catering, especially for full-day events, along with any necessary permits or insurance, are included in the infrastructure needed to host a successful seminar. Given the number of moving parts, it is not recommended to attempt an in-person event right out of the gate on your own.

The alternative is creating an online course. Delivery is made through one of the many reliable online course platforms that supports multimedia content. Most business-school professors are familiar with this kind of delivery, having worked with their own university's learning-management systems like Blackboard, Canvas, and Moodle. By transforming your solution frameworks into a structured online course, and delivering it through a commercial-course platform, you can potentially deliver your programming on a global scale.

In the world of online courses, there's a classification system that typically includes what is referred to as a low-tier course, priced under $200. Topics like "Digital Marketing" and "Introduction to SEO: Tactics and Strategy for Entrepreneurs" or "Going Freelance: Building Your Own Business" are typical of this price range. Let's say you develop a low-tier course and price it at $197. If you manage to sell just 42 enrollments a month, you would generate nearly $100,000 per year and double our average professor's salary.

On the other hand, high-tier programs, which are considered high-value, can be priced around $2,000 per course. High-tier online business courses are typically more comprehensive, offering in-depth insights and often including interactive components like live sessions and networking opportunities. Many times these courses are facilitated by renowned institutions like Harvard or Wharton, or leading industry experts, but they are broad topics—like negotiation or project management—aimed at a broad audience. Academic authorities can create more specialized courses aimed at audiences often overlooked by prestigious programs but nonetheless willing to pay for high-value solutions. If you were to create such a program and charge $1,997, selling just four enrollments a month would generate nearly $100,000 a year.

It's important to note that there are costs associated with creating and hosting these programs, but numerous hosting companies can manage the transactional aspects, such as processing payments and delivering the course to participants. You don't need technical skills like coding; these platforms handle the logistics for a fee. Your primary responsibility is to create your frameworks and market your program effectively to encourage enrollment.

Coaching and Consulting

Finally, coaching and consulting present valuable pathways for academic thought leaders to be compensated for their expertise.

Coaching, in this context, involves guiding clients through personal or professional development, leveraging your insights to foster growth, enhance skills, and achieve specific goals. This personalized approach not only allows authorities to apply their knowledge in diverse scenarios but also to witness the direct impact of their expertise on individuals' careers and lives. The intimate nature of coaching, coupled with the bespoke application of your frameworks, makes it highly rewarding for academics seeking to make a difference on a personal level, while also receiving fair compensation for their specialized services.

Consulting, on the other hand, offers a broader platform for authorities to influence organizational strategies, operational efficiencies, and overall performance. As consultants, thought leaders can engage with various organizations, from corporate entities to nonprofits, providing expert analysis, recommending evidence-based solutions, and assisting with the implementation of new policies or procedures. This role not only underscores the practical value of your frameworks in solving complex industry challenges but also establishes you as an indispensable resource in their field. Moreover, consulting engagements often lead to significant financial returns, reflecting the high value placed on expert advice in today's competitive business environment.

The potential earnings from coaching and consulting as an academic thought leader can vary widely based on factors such as expertise, reputation, market demand, and the specific arrangements made with clients. Executive-coaching fees can range from $200 to $500 per hour for coaches with moderate experience or who are working with mid-level executives. Highly experienced coaches, particularly those working with senior executives or C-suite leaders, can command hourly rates of $500 to more than $1,000. Many executive coaches offer coaching packages that span several months and can include a set number of sessions, assessments, and support materials. These packages can range from $3,000 to $10,000, with more comprehensive, long-term engagements reaching $15,000 to $50,000 or more. Some executive coaches work on a retainer basis, providing ongoing support, guidance, and availability over a set period, typically ranging from $2,000 to $10,000 per month. High-end coaches working with top executives or on complex organizational challenges may charge significantly higher retainers.

As an example, if you are an academic with expertise in leadership development, you might offer executive-coaching services. If you charge $250 per hour and engage with clients for two sessions per month over a six-month period, a single client could generate $3,000. Working with thirty clients a year, this would amount to nearly $100,000 in additional income. If you were able to charge $500 per hour, you would need about 16 clients. By moving up the seniority ladder to the C-suite and charging $1,000 per hour, you would need only a handful of clients each year to double the average professor's salary.

Consulting fees also range substantially. For example, an academic specializing in business strategy might consult for a corporation looking to enter a new market. For a three-month project, they could charge a flat fee of $50,000, including an initial assessment, strategy formulation, and implementation. Alternatively, an academic authority in innovation and entrepreneurship might work with startups on a retainer basis, providing ongoing advice and support. A monthly retainer fee of $3,000 over 12 months from just one startup would total $36,000. And finally, an academic expert in regulatory policy might secure an annual contract with a government agency to advise on economic-policy development and analysis. A contract valued at $100,000 for the year could involve regular meetings, report preparations, and policy briefings.

These examples illustrate the breadth of opportunities available for academic thought leaders in coaching and consulting. Earnings can range from supplemental income to significant sums that may surpass academic salaries, depending on the scope of the work, the number of clients or projects taken on, and the thought leader's standing in their field. It's important for academics to assess their unique value proposition, market demand for their expertise, and the best channels through which to offer their services to maximize their earning potential.

Capturing Your Share of the Value You Create

This chapter has given you an overview of the ways you can package your solution frameworks and offer them to your audience for compensation. We've looked at how each one of them could conceivably generate an additional income of $100,000 per year, the equivalent of the average business-school faculty salary. Let's sum up:

1. You begin by creating a digital book and selling directly to your audience through your website at a price of $49.95. If you sell 165 copies each month, you generate **$98,901** per year.

2. With your published book and honed platform skills, you are booking keynote speeches at $8,000 per engagement. If you give one speech per month, you generate another **$96,000** per year.

3. In addition to speaking, you have created a training webinar and priced it at the low end for $99. By offering the webinar just once per month and attracting 80 attendees, you generate about **$95,040** per year.

4. You have also created a low-tier online course, priced under $197. You sell 42 enrollments a month, generating **$99,288**.

5. You also have developed your signature high-end online course that you price at $997; by selling just 10 enrollments a month, you generate nearly **$119,640** a year.

With just these five activities you have been able to generate more than half-a-million dollars a year in additional income. Beyond this could include coaching and consulting engagements. And, of course, these are not separate, isolated activities. They are derived from a single asset that they mutually share: your solution frameworks. Thus, they support one another synergistically. Someone may buy your book and then want to learn more and sign up for your online course. Or someone may attend your webinar, see you presenting and decide that you would be a great speaker for their upcoming conference. Your different offerings can be mixed and matched, depending on the needs of your audience and clients. And, because they are all based on a common foundation, they do not disperse your attention and energies, but allow you to focus on your content and community.

Final Thoughts and Capturing Value

As discussed, compensation is often a delicate topic. However, for academic authorities, financial rewards are secondary and are a natural and fair consequence of the value they create. When you dedicate yourself to solving pressing problems for practitioners, crafting actionable frameworks, and sharing insights that improve organizational performance, fair compensation follows. It reflects the tangible impact of your work on the communities you serve, affirming your authority's relevance and effectiveness.

Capturing Your Share of Your Created Value

The examples given here illustrate what some thought leaders achieve, but the true reward lies not in financial gain. It lies in the contributions you make to practice, the growth you witness in your community, and the personal growth and satisfaction you experience. By stepping into a leadership role, you help others achieve their goals and facilitate meaningful change. This mantle of leadership offers an intrinsic reward that transcends material measures. The financial rewards enhance your ability to live a secure and adventurous life, care for your loved ones, and build a fulfilling retirement. Through this journey, you elevate your field and leave a legacy—a testament to the lives you've impacted and inspired.

• • •

AFTERWORD
Authority in a Complex World

We've covered a lot of ground in this book, tracing the contours of how to become an academic authority and what that means for you and your field of expertise. From the mindset and motivations that drive the journey, to the steps for engaging communities, solving meaningful problems, and crafting solutions, you now have the tools to create your own path and take the steps toward building your unique legacy as a thought leader.

The decision to act is yours. This is not a journey of instant gratification, but one of steady progress, impact, and fulfillment. It is a commitment to transforming your expertise into influence and your passion into purpose. The next chapter isn't just in this book; it's in your life—becoming the authority the world demands.

Today's world needs thought leaders like never before. The complexity of global challenges—whether in management, strategy, or society at large—demands voices grounded in both rigorous academic insight and practical solutions. You, as an academic thought leader, are uniquely positioned to meet these challenges and make a lasting impact.

Becoming an authority is not a "get rich quick" scheme. It is a path of personal and professional growth, requiring patience, persistence, and a genuine commitment to advancing understanding while providing tangible benefits to your audience. Along the way, as you hone your expertise and gain recognition, you will experience both intrinsic rewards—such as the satisfaction of contributing to your field—and extrinsic rewards in the form of recognition, influence, and a more secure future.

The steps in this book have been designed to get you to the liftoff stage and help you establish a sustainable thought-leadership platform. As you grow, your work will not only enrich your own life but also provide the resources and flexibility to support the people you care about.

The world needs your voice. Take the lessons of this book, and apply them. Start small, engage with your community, and build your solutions. Each step forward will bring you closer to becoming the influential thought leader the world needs.

Remember, authority is not just about possessing knowledge; it's about using that knowledge to inspire, lead, and make a difference. It's time to step into your role as a true academic authority. The journey to your legacy begins now.

• • •

ABOUT THE AUTHOR
Dr. Gregory Unruh

Dr. Gregory Unruh is an authority in sustainability strategy and an expert in the field of corporate responsibility and environmental innovation. Founder of the Arison Professorship at George Mason University, Dr. Unruh has dedicated his career to bridging the gap between academic research and practical solutions in the realm of sustainable business practices. In addition to *Academic Authority: The Professor's Guide to Becoming a Sought-After Thought Leader*, he is the author of *The Biosphere Rules: Nature's Five Circularity Secrets for Sustainable Profits* and *Strategy on the Sustainability Frontier: Creating Business Value and Contributing to a Better World*, and the co-author of *Being Global: How to Think, Act, and Lead in a Transformed World* published by Harvard Business Review Press.

He first rose to prominence with his "Carbon Lock-In" theory, which illuminates the systemic challenges of transitioning industries to cleaner technologies. This theory has been influential in shaping environmental policy and corporate strategies aimed at combating climate change and won Academy of Management recognition as one of the most influential articles in business sustainability.

Dr. Unruh began his thought-leadership journey by authoring some of the first management frameworks in the emerging field of sustainable business practices. His early work helped define how companies could integrate sustainability into their core operations, long before it became a mainstream business imperative. A prolific writer, Dr. Unruh has published extensively in academic journals and top practitioner outlets, including the *Harvard Business Review*, *MIT Sloan Management Review*, and *Forbes*.

Beyond his academic achievements, Dr. Unruh is passionate about equipping fellow scholars with the tools they need to become academic authorities in their own right. His work on thought leadership emphasizes the importance of connecting academic expertise with practical applications, allowing scholars to create lasting impact.

Dr. Unruh holds a PhD from the Fletcher School of Law and Diplomacy and has taught at leading institutions around the world, including Columbia University, Thunderbird School of Global Management, Olin School of Business at Washington University, IE Business School, Egade at Tech de Monterey, INCAE Business School in Costa Rica, and the Rotterdam School of Management. When he's not helping organizations tackle sustainability challenges, he is actively engaged in mentoring the next generation of leaders working for positive change.

About the Author

About Global Leadership Academy

This book is proudly published by Global Leadership Academy Press, a division of the Global Leadership Academy (GLA). GLA is committed to empowering academics to become influential thought leaders who bridge the gap between scholarly insight and practical application. With a mission to inspire and equip academics to transcend traditional boundaries, GLA provides the tools and strategies needed to share transformative knowledge with the world.

Through its publishing arm, including works like *Academic Authority*, GLA supports scholars in amplifying their voices and creating real-world impact. Beyond publishing, GLA offers a suite of resources and programs designed to guide academics on their thought-leadership journey, from building authority platforms to engaging practitioner communities.

To learn more about GLA's offerings, including bonus video trainings and exclusive content for aspiring thought leaders, please visit www.global-leadershipacademy.com.

The Academic Authority Online Training Program

If you've enjoyed this book and are interested in taking the next step in your journey toward thought leadership, we invite you to explore a deeper, more comprehensive training opportunity. The Academic Authority Online Training Program was designed to build on the principles outlined in these pages, providing you with the tools and support needed to fully realize your potential as an academic authority. Whether you're just starting out or looking to refine your impact, this program offers the guidance you need.

The Academic Authority Online Training Program is a comprehensive, self-paced course designed to guide scholars through every stage of becoming a thought leader in their field. Offered by the Global Leadership Academy, this one of a kind program provides the strategies, tools, and actionable steps you need to build your authority platform, engage practitioner audiences, and create a lasting impact both inside and outside academia.

This program is built on the principles outlined in *Academic Authority* and features exclusive video modules, interactive worksheets, a resource library, and access to expert insights. At a list price of $2,995, participants will gain access to the lifetime of the curriculum that covers everything from developing your unique perspective and crafting solutions to communicating effectively with broader audiences.

To get started, sign up for our Academic Authority Mini Course, where you'll receive complimentary foundational lessons along with special discount offers for the full program.

Learn more and enroll today at:
www.globalleadershipacademy.com

www.ingramcontent.com/pod-product-compliance
Lightning Source LLC
Chambersburg PA
CBHW081506080526
44589CB00017B/2670